AF469014

DRAWN IN COLOUR
DEGAS FROM THE BURRELL COLLECTION

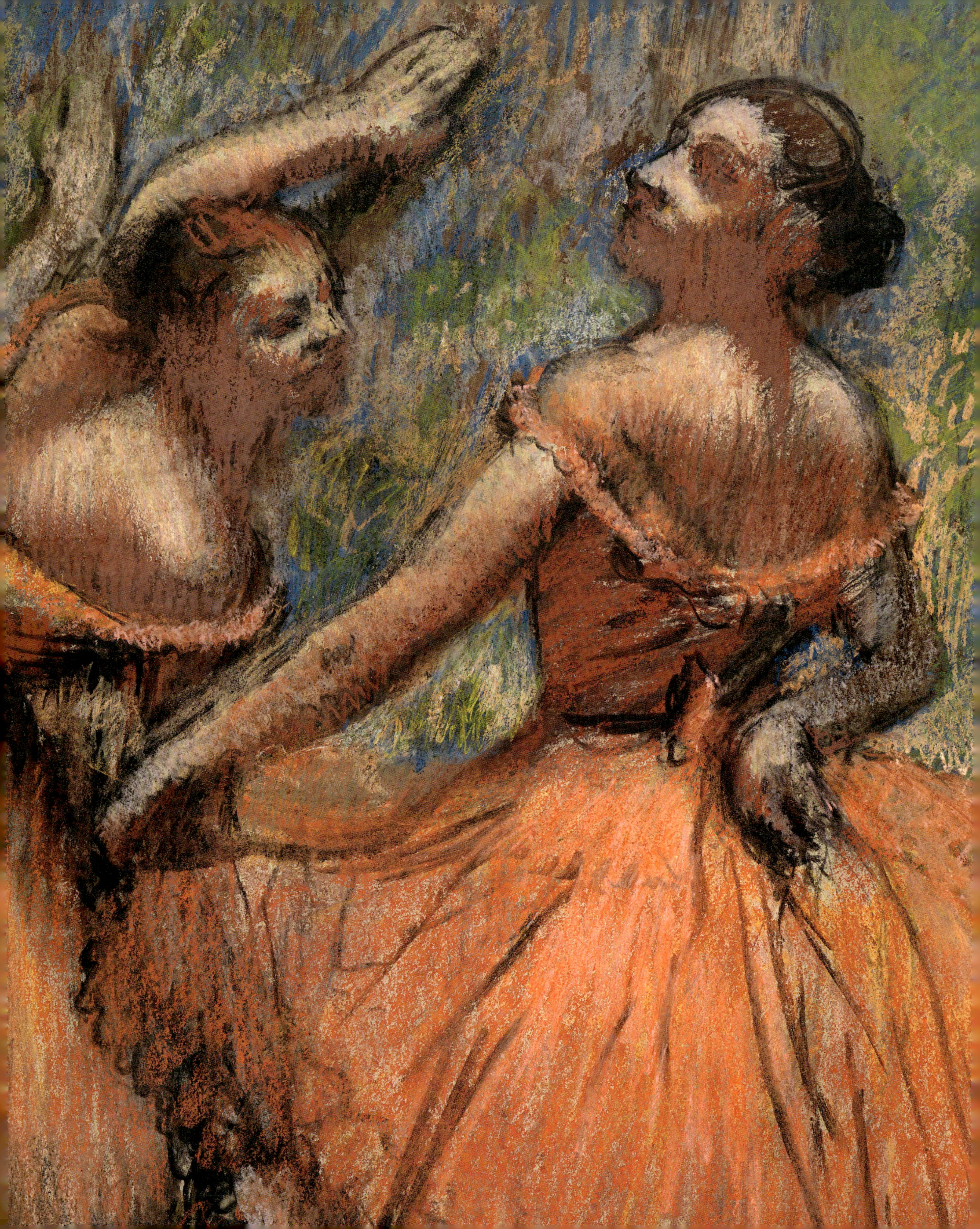

DRAWN IN COLOUR

DEGAS FROM THE BURRELL COLLECTION

VIVIEN HAMILTON

WITH JULIEN DOMERCQ AND HARRIET K. STRATIS

CONTRIBUTIONS BY SARAH HERRING
AND CHRISTOPHER RIOPELLE

National Gallery Company, London
Distributed by Yale University Press

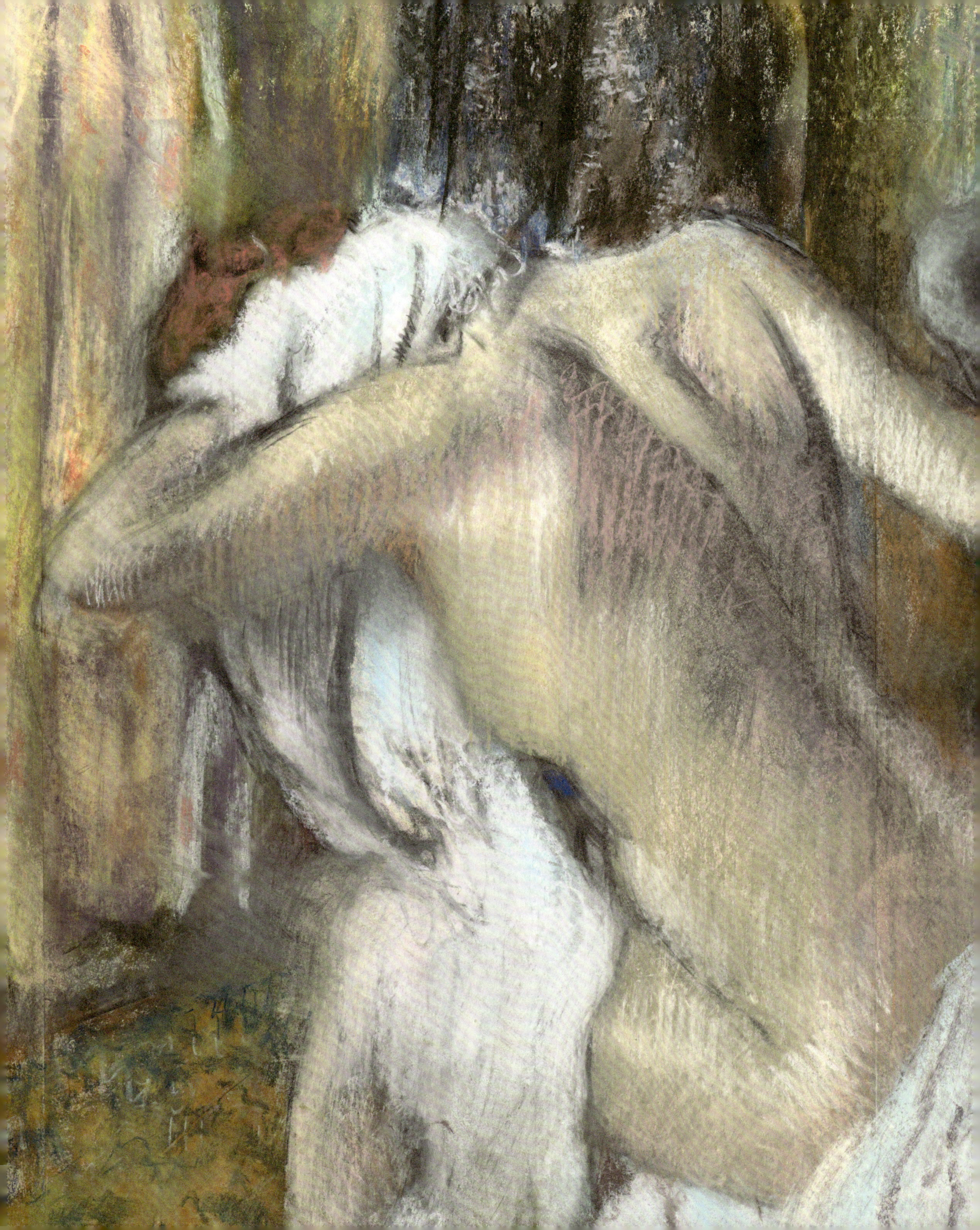

CONTENTS

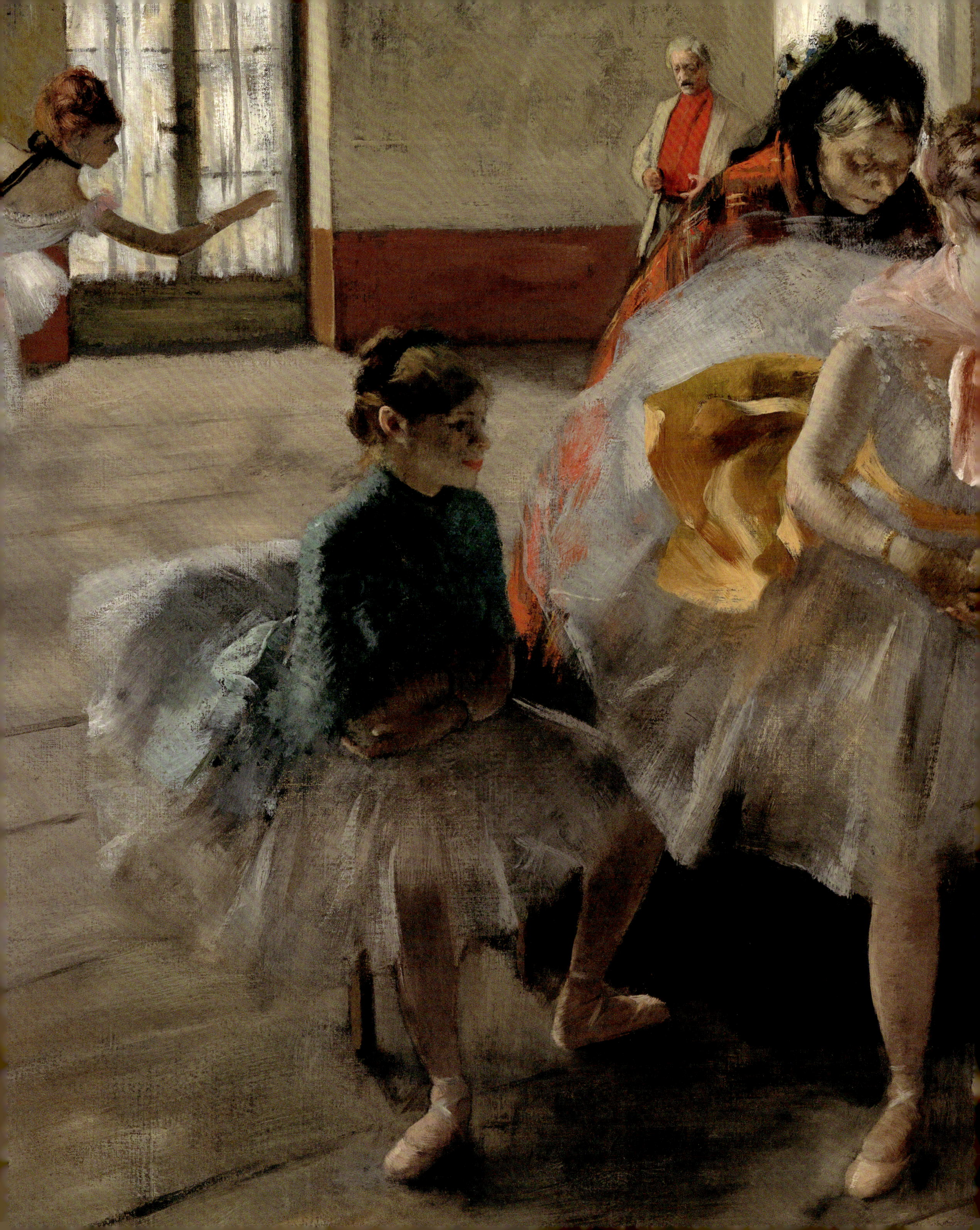

DIRECTORS' FOREWORD

Edgar Degas died exactly one hundred years ago on 27 September 1917. The National Gallery is marking the centenary by exhibiting the collection of paintings and pastels by the artist formed by the Scottish shipping magnate, Sir William Burrell (1861–1958). In 1944 in one of the most generous acts of public patronage this country has ever seen, Burrell and his wife, Constance Mitchell, donated to the city of Glasgow, the place of his birth, almost 9000 works of art, including paintings, drawings, sculptures, stained glass, arms and armour, furniture and tapestries. The building which houses them in Pollok Country Park is currently undergoing a major refurbishment programme, enabling this display to take place.

The Burrell's Degas collection is made up of 22 paintings, pastels and drawings which reflect the arc of his career and the subjects that obsessed him, dancers, horse racing, scenes from modern life and women at their toilette. The exhibition is the largest selection of those works ever to be shown together outside Scotland; it also includes the pastel of *Russian Dancers* which Burrell donated to the Berwick-upon-Tweed Museum and Art Gallery in 1949 and a small number of works from the National Gallery's collection that serve to articulate and enrich the display.

Degas always stood slightly apart from his Impressionist colleagues. His lack of interest in plein-air painting, his abiding passion for the art of the great masters, and his experimentation in different media, including photography, made his art intensely personal. As he got older and his eyesight became weaker, his palette became ever more brilliant and his use of pastels on paper enabled him to achieve levels of searing chromatic intensity which have rarely been paralleled either by his contemporaries or his successors. A hundred years on, Degas's legacy as an artist committed to the pursuit of beauty through constant experiment and an incessant devotion to his craft continue to inspire awed admiration.

This exhibition has been made possible thanks to the generosity of the Trustees of the Burrell Collection and Glasgow Life. We are grateful to the sponsor, Groupe Eurotunnel, the Elizabeth Cayzer Charitable Trust, Colin Clark and other benefactors for their support. We also want to put on record our gratitude to colleagues at the Burrell and at the National Gallery.

Gabriele Finaldi
Director, The National Gallery

James Robinson
Director, Burrell Renaissance

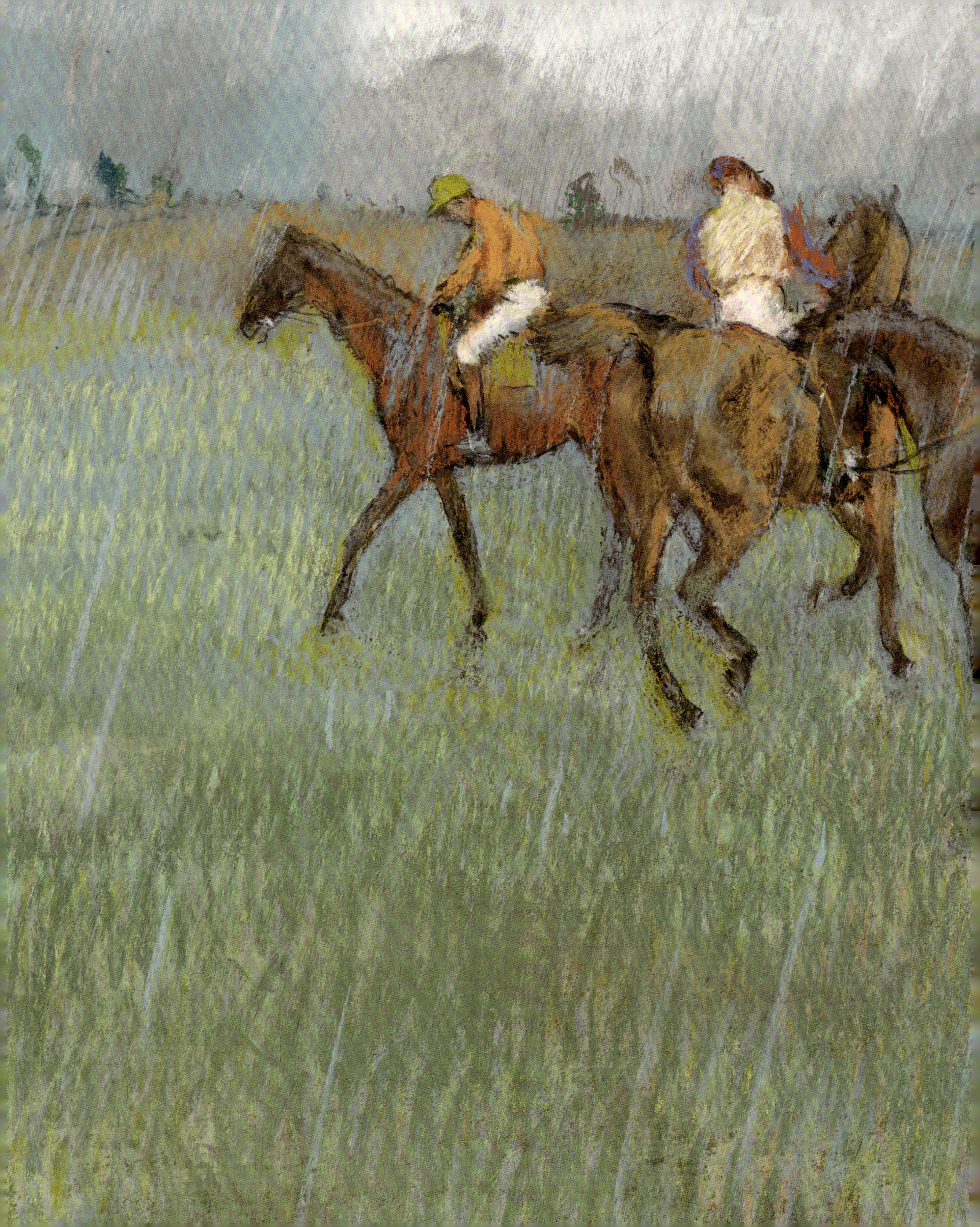

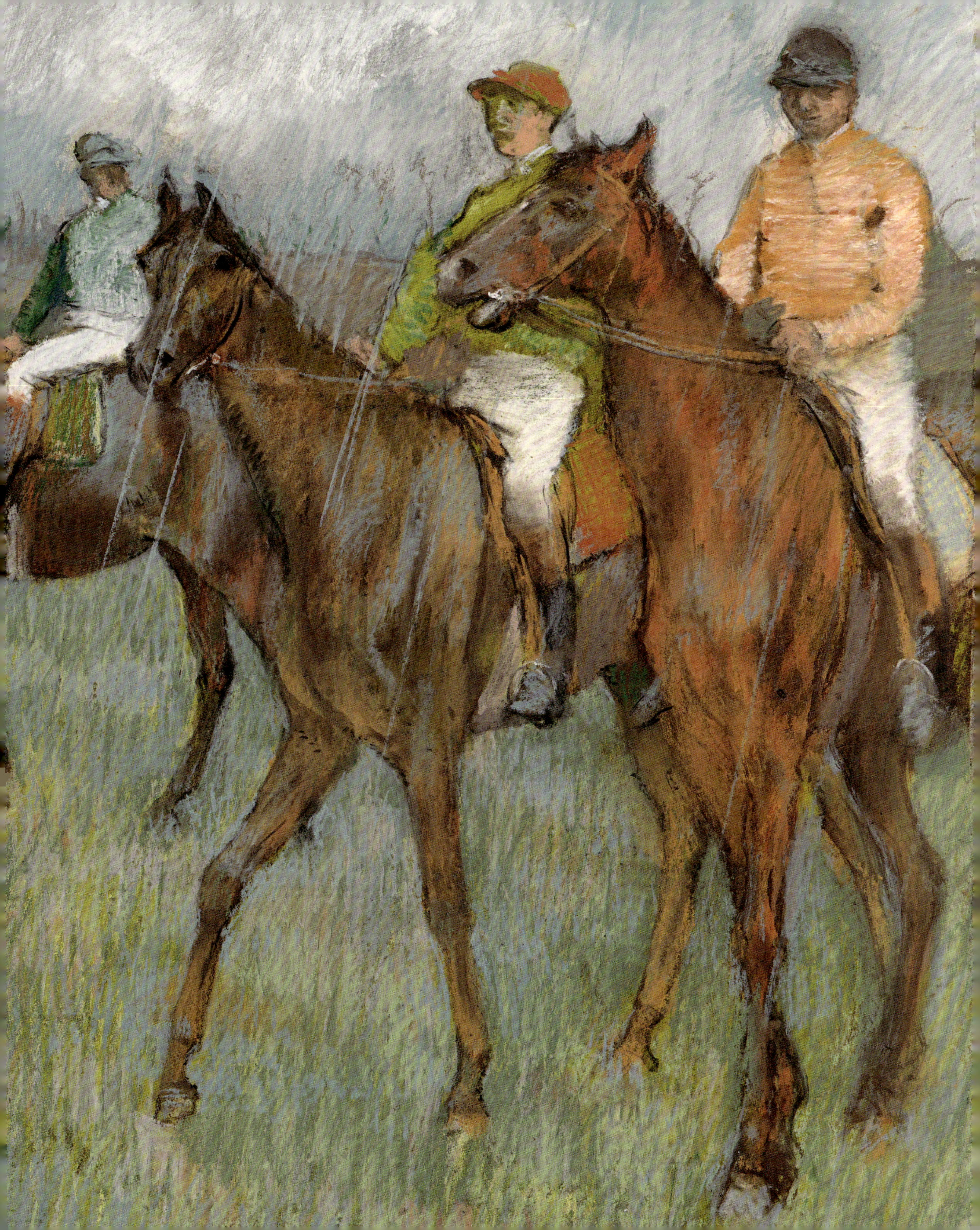

EDGAR DEGAS: RELENTLESSLY MOVING AHEAD

JULIEN DOMERCQ

EMERGING from the shadows of a page of brown paper, in a few quick and masterful strokes of paint, a young woman looks straight at us through a pair of binoculars (cat. 1). Her gaze is direct, powerful and assertive. Despite the work's small size, she has a monumental presence. Dressed in an elegant red and black dress, she uses her left hand to steady her right arm holding the binoculars, so we can be in no doubt that she will be able to hold our gaze. Her face is partially in shadow but bright enough to reveal the hint of a quietly confident smile. Who is she looking at? Surely she is following a horse taking part in a race before her. However much we remind ourselves that she is just a sketch for a figure intended to be part of a larger horseracing composition, we cannot help but be puzzled by her presence and the power of her gaze. She becomes the embodiment of the act of looking itself. Such is the power of the art of Edgar Degas.

Degas (1834–1917) sketched *Woman looking through Field Glasses* around 1869, in his mid-thirties, at a time when he and his friend Edouard Manet (1832–1883) followed the elegant Parisian crowds to the new racecourses that had recently been built on the outskirts of the capital. A founding member of the group that became known as the Impressionists, Degas pursued a remarkably

Detail of cat. 1

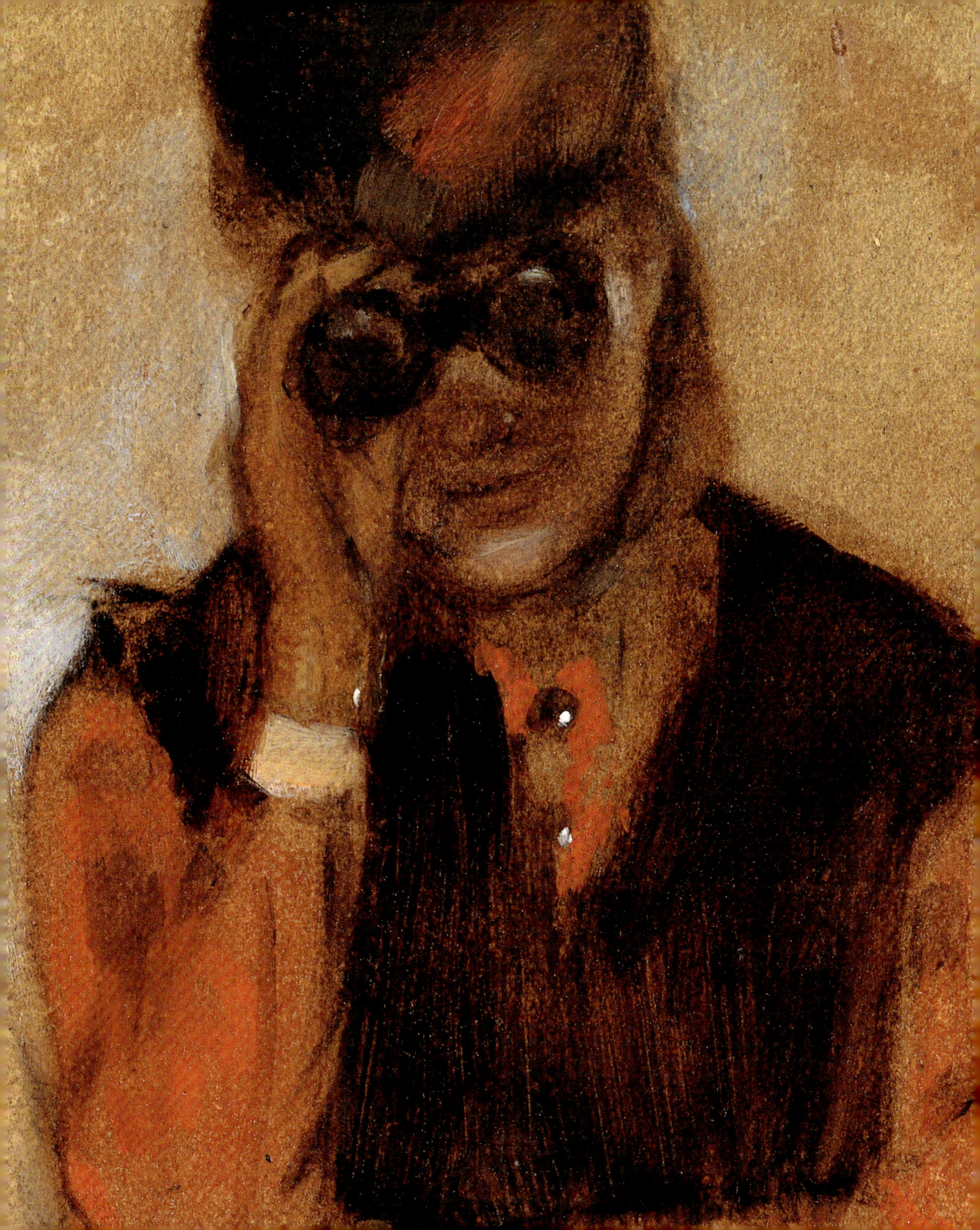

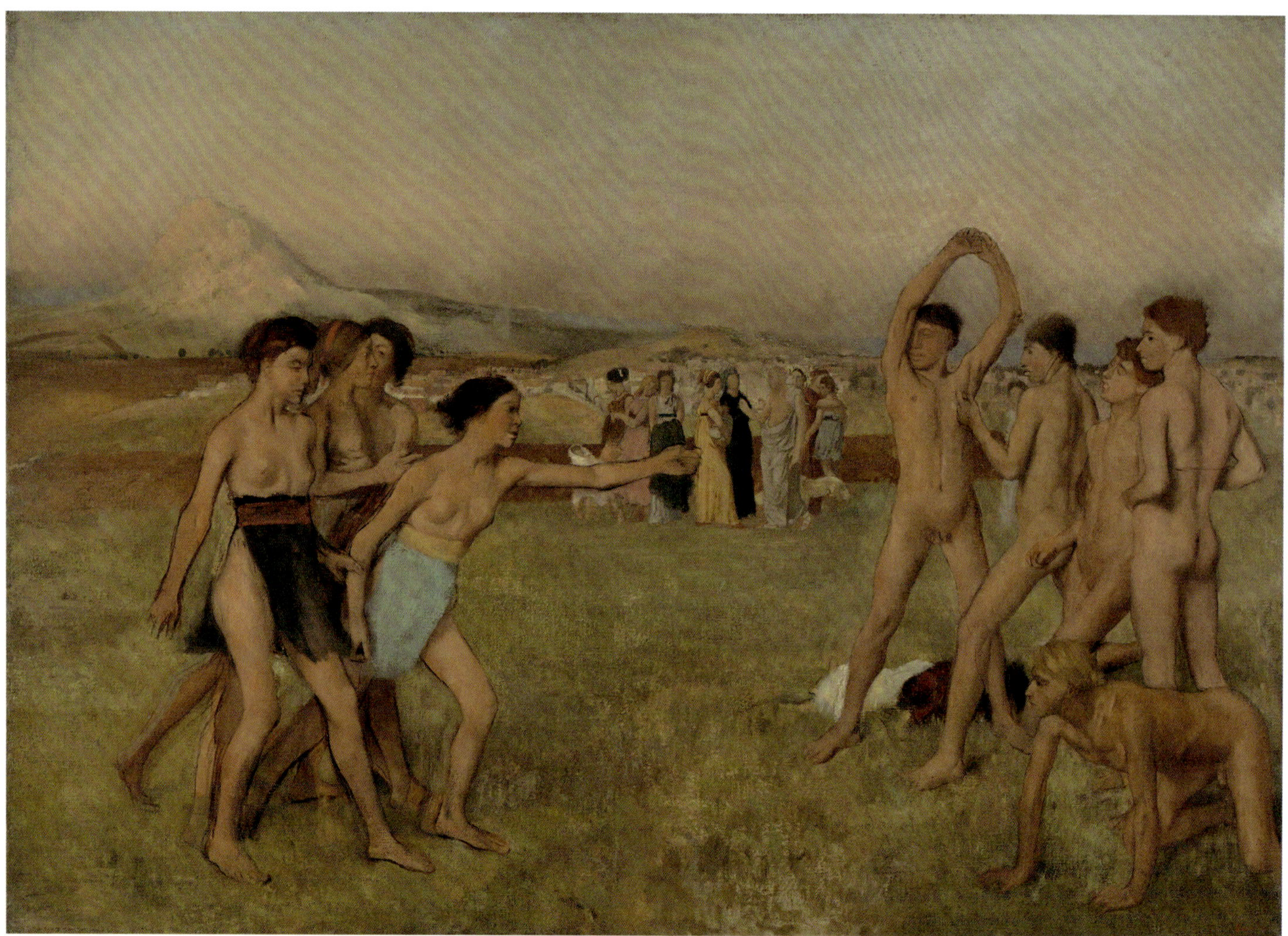

Fig. 1
Edgar Degas (1834–1917)
Young Spartans exercising,
about 1860
Oil on canvas, 109.5 × 155 cm
The National Gallery, London
NG 3860

individual vision, distinct from that of his fellow artists. While they mainly painted in oils, Degas feverishly experimented with media, pushing the boundaries of techniques as varied as oil painting, pastel, drawing, printmaking, sculpture and even photography. Unlike other Impressionists, who were drawn to painting the world as they encountered it out of doors, Degas despised plein-air painting, telling his dealer Ambroise Vollard (1866–1939) in his characteristic acerbic, tongue-in-cheek way: 'If I were the government I would have a special brigade of gendarmes to keep an eye on artists who paint landscapes from nature. Oh, I don't mean to kill anyone; just a little dose of bird-shot now and then as a warning.'[1] While an Impressionist such as Pierre-Auguste Renoir (1841–1919) moved quickly from one motif to another, rarely repeating himself, Degas delighted in returning, time and time again, to specific visual problems: how to depict the tension in the neck of a recalcitrant horse pulling on its bridle (cat. 4); the painful strain in a dancer's foot after hours of rehearsals (cat. 18); or the uncomfortable twist in the back of a woman attempting to dry herself after the bath (cat. 26).

This deep sense of individuality was already present in the early stages of his career. Degas did not complete his studies at the Ecole des Beaux-Arts, the bastion of academic painting, but instead embarked on two self-funded trips to Italy: first in 1856 and again in 1858–9. There he followed the advice that he later claimed Jean-Auguste-Dominique Ingres (1780–1867) had given him: 'draw lines ... lots of lines, either from memory or from nature'.[2] During extended stays in Naples, Rome and Florence, Degas filled the pages of his notebooks with sketches from life and of the great works of antiquity and the Renaissance. Aspiring to emulate the old masters, Degas imagined he would follow the respectable path of history painting, which was considered to be at the very top of the hierarchy of artistic genres: large, learned compositions filled with figures of the ancient or medieval past.

One of Degas's few history paintings ever to have made it beyond myriad preparatory drawings and oil sketches is *Young Spartans exercising,* painted around 1860 (fig. 1). Degas had a particular affection towards this work, which held pride of place in his studio well into the twentieth century. Its subject matter was unconventional: he chose to depict a rather obscure passage from the Greek philosopher Plutarch, detailing the manly upbringing of Spartan girls. This work does more to bring in the contemporary world than first meets the eye. Aside from its classical subject matter, *Young Spartans* also evokes nascent adolescent sexuality and the meeting of the sexes on an equal footing. Degas's Spartan youths are not idealised classical bodies inspired by the Antique sculptures he knew so well, but contemporary Parisian types transposed into a scene from ancient Greece. One can recognise the svelte little bodies of his future dancers in the Spartan girls, while his boys appear to be modelled on youths from Montmartre, where he lived.[3] Under the respectable veneer of the classical, we can already decipher a keen interest in the modern world that surrounded him.

Similarly, his *Scene of War in the Middle Ages* (fig. 2), exhibited at the Salon of 1865, seems to have been a pretext for observing the nude female body. A mysterious and terrifying *essence* painting – a medium often used by Degas in which he drained paint of its oil before diluting it with turpentine – it represents nine naked women breathing their last breath, on a dusty road in open countryside, at the mercy of three archers. These are the bodies of real contemporary women, exposed, contorted, tortured even, foreshadowing the multiple iterations of the poses of dancers and

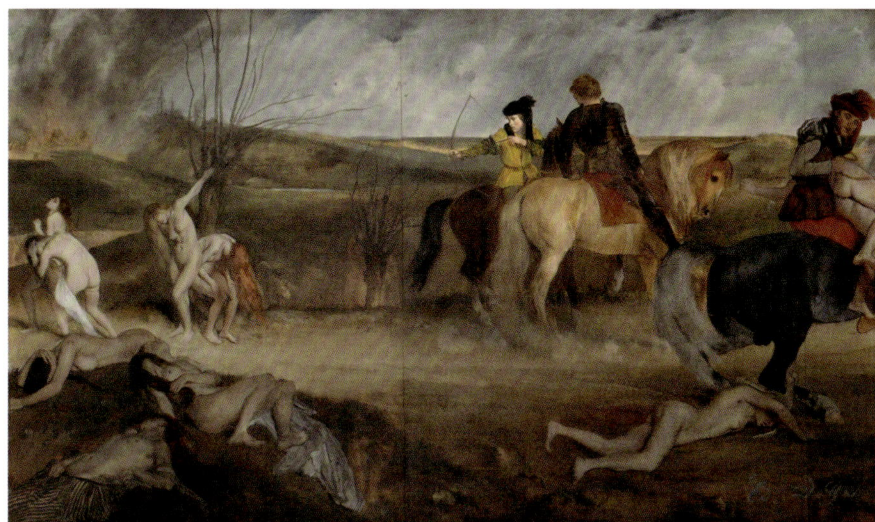

Fig. 2
Edgar Degas (1834–1917)
Scene of War in the Middle Ages,
about 1865
Oil and *essence* on paper,
83.5 × 148.5 cm
Musée d'Orsay, Paris
RF 2208

bathers that were to become Degas's staple. In the words of his friend the art critic Edmond Duranty (1833–1880), Degas's early historical work was already burning with the 'fire of contemporary life'.[4]

Degas's sojourn in Italy also constituted a homecoming of sorts for him: his paternal grandfather had made a fortune as a banker in Naples, after allegedly narrowly escaping the guillotine during the French Revolution. Degas spent the most part of 1858 in Florence staying at the home of his beloved aunt, Laura, and her husband, Gennaro Bellelli, who was discontentedly living in political exile. There Degas began working on his first masterpiece, *The Bellelli Family*, completed in 1867 (fig. 3), which established him as one of the most incisive portraitists of his age. While family portraits usually aimed to emphasise family unity, here Degas 'wanted to paint – and stubbornly perfected – the portrait of a family united by reciprocal aversions'.[5] On the grand scale of aristocratic portraits, Degas represents, in a contemporary bourgeois interior, a family in turmoil: his aunt Laura slowly consumed by depression, with her gaze 'so fixed and absent as to make her seem blind'. She stares into the void, past the figure of her indifferent, bitter husband, while one of their daughters looks defiantly at us and the other sits uncomfortably and precariously between her parents. The culmination of Degas's work as a portraitist can be seen in his 1879 portrait of Edmond Duranty (cat. 2). A modern portrait *par excellence*, it depicts Duranty in the 'modern' manner he advocated, at his desk in his everyday clothes, surrounded by the instruments of his trade: a multitude of coloured books, scribbled pages, magnifying glasses, pens and a bottle of ink.

By the late 1870s, however, portraiture had become the exception rather than the rule in Degas's work, and the artist had long turned his back on history painting, focusing on representing the Parisian world that surrounded him, a world that was changing at an unprecedented speed. The industrial revolution had drawn in huge numbers from the countryside, triggering massive urban expansion. Modernisation projects begun under Napoleon III led to the reconstruction of entire districts, some of them pierced by grand boulevards, and the creation of places of leisure such as parks, racecourses and the great opera house designed by architect Charles Garnier. Before his eyes, Paris was transforming into the first modern metropolis, Walter Benjamin's 'capital of the nineteenth century'.[6] Degas's new artist friends of the 1860s, such as Manet and Renoir, shared his fascination for this new world, a whirlwind of colour, a metropolis in constant flux illuminated by artificial light which changed the very nature of vision itself. Rapidly, Degas's art filled with depictions of the highs and lows of Parisian life: elegant men and women animating the cafés lining the city's new boulevards (cat. 8) as well as exhausted young laundresses slaving away in subterranean workrooms (cat. 9). To depict the modern world, he developed new modes of representation. For instance, his exquisite *In the Tuileries Gardens* painted about 1880 (cat. 7), is deeply indebted to photography, capturing in an instant – perhaps through the window of an omnibus – the blur of a woman's face. In these works Degas suggests being part of the shifting Parisian crowd, observing and being observed.

One aspect of modern Parisian life captivated him more than any other: the ballet. The Paris Opéra played an important role in the lives of the new upper middle classes of which Degas was part – it was as much a place to watch ballet or opera as a place to watch others and to be watched. Degas lived and worked a few streets away, in the quarter known as 'La Nouvelle Athènes', and enthusiastically visited

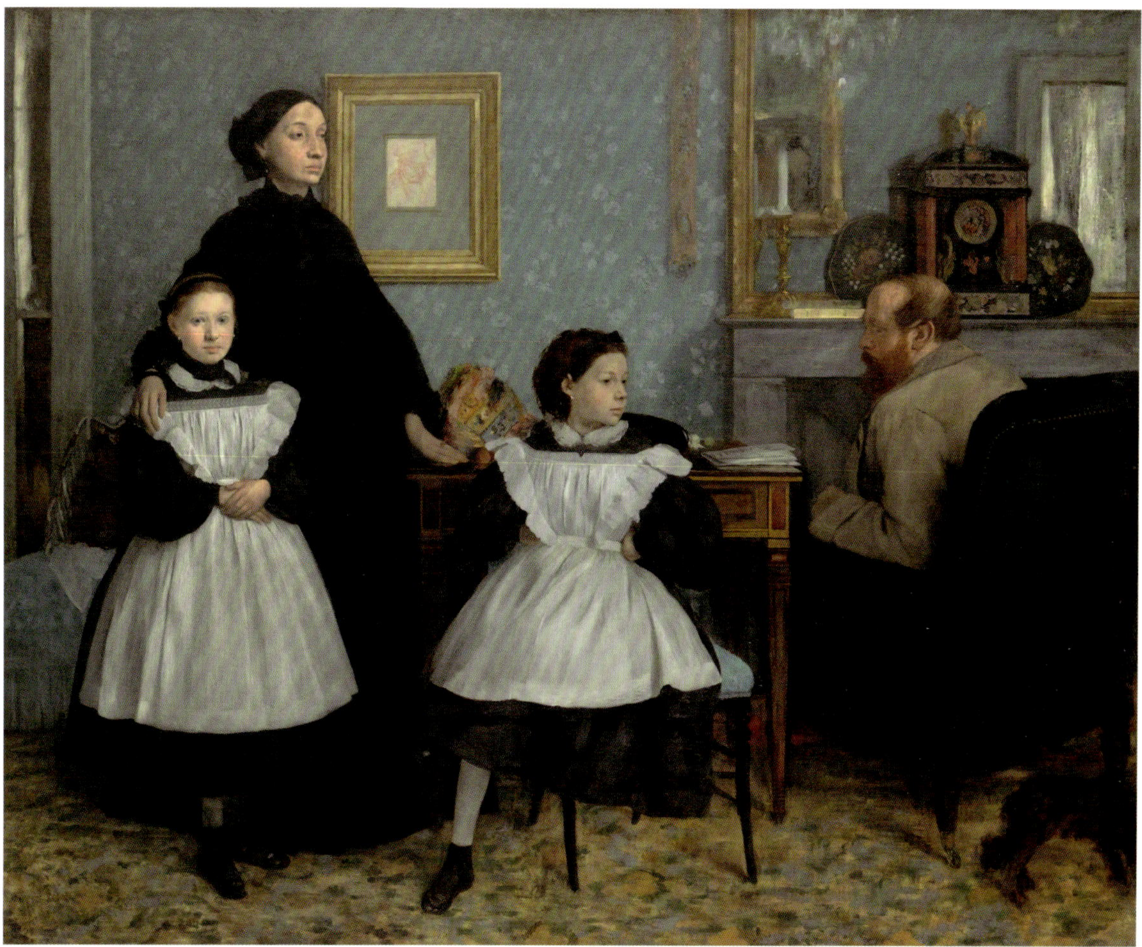

Fig. 3
Edgar Degas (1834–1917)
Family Portrait, also called
The Bellelli Family, about 1867
Oil on canvas, 201 × 249.5 cm
Musée d'Orsay, Paris
RF 2210

the Opéra. Surviving records show that between 1885 and 1892, he attended performances there on no fewer than 117 evenings, and from around 1882 he was granted much-coveted backstage access.[7]

Degas's first dancers appeared in the background of *The Orchestra of the Opéra* (fig. 4) painted about 1870. Commissioned by bassoonist Désiré Dihau (1833–1909), the work is a portrait of a man practising his art, surrounded by other portraits of his orchestra colleagues. It is symptomatic of Degas's intimate knowledge of the world of the Opéra, the artist positioning himself in the first row, on the very edge of the orchestra pit. Our eye is drawn upwards, however, beyond the balding heads of the musicians, the prancing violin bows and the scroll of a double base, to the very edge of the picture where the stage's footlights reveal disembodied ballerinas, their legs and tutus merging in a whirlwind of colour and movement.

It is tempting to see the almost accidental appearance of ballerinas on the edge of this painting as the moment when Degas might have realised that he could make the popular theme of life in and around Paris's elegant Opéra uniquely his own. While other contemporary representations of the Opéra depicted its renowned extravagant stage sets or its high society gatherings in the theatre's grand foyers, Degas's interest rapidly shifted onto the dancers themselves. He rarely depicted them on stage and more often focused on their waiting in the wings (cats 16, 17) or taking

Fig. 4
Edgar Degas (1834–1917)
The Orchestra of the Opéra, about 1870
Oil on canvas, 56.5 × 46 cm
Musée d'Orsay, Paris
RF 2417

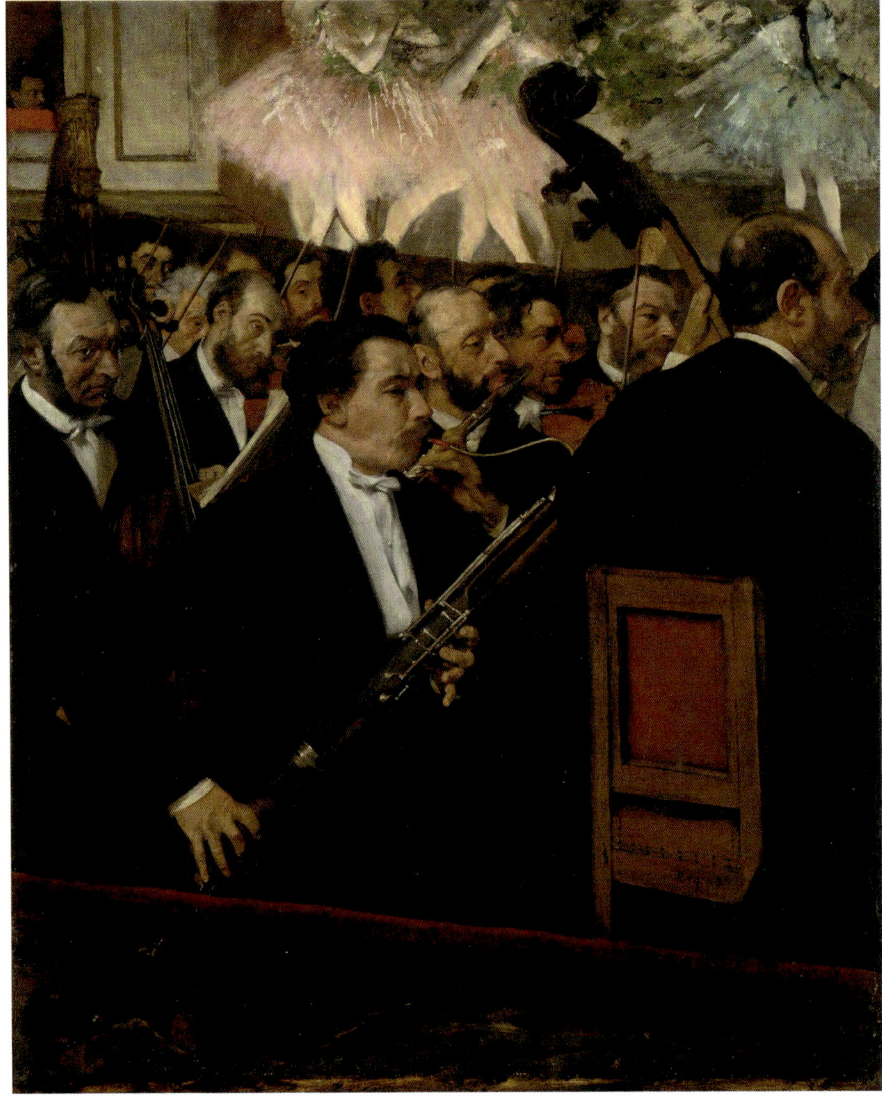

part in rehearsals (cats 13, 14). Far from the gilded world of the spectators, Degas chose to depict the gritty reality of life backstage. There, young, impoverished ballerinas from humble backgrounds spent hours rehearsing to attain perfection, their limbs sore, jostling for the attention of their dance masters, and all too frequently prostituting themselves to high society gentlemen so that they could afford to stay in competition for coveted stardom. However, while these preying men in black frock coats and top hats sometimes appear on the margins of his pictures, Degas's real interest in the secret world of ballet dancers was that it gave him a chance to study a near-infinite range of crude or sophisticated but always complex movements: from a ballerina's graceful *allongés* or arabesques to her tired body stretching or prostrate on a bench following her efforts.

One of his first autonomous ballet works was *The Rehearsal* (cat. 11), produced around the time of the groundbreaking First Impressionist Exhibition of 1874. It is as if one has just stumbled into a bustling rehearsal room, unnoticed by all but the watchful eye of dance master Jules Perrot in the background. Despite giving a sense of immediacy, the work is actually the product of the combination of individually observed studies carefully put together to create a whole, coherent composition. The crop is particularly daring and once again seems indebted to photography: the dancer at the front of the composition is cut in half by the right side of the picture, while at the top left the disembodied limbs of dancers come down the winding staircase. The centre of the picture is left strikingly bare, filled by the diagonals of the floorboards.

Degas's interest in the ballet coincided with his first serious forays into the medium of pastel. The Burrell Collection holds one of his earliest pastels of this subject, *Preparation for the Class* (cat. 12), created around 1877, its silvery and carefully blended tones still indebted to the grand tradition of French eighteenth-century pastel. Degas relished the variety of informal poses of the dancers, some comforted by their mothers, leading the viewer's eye around the dark room which is lit by a window overlooking the rooftops of Paris. At first practising what contemporaries termed 'scientific realism' in his depictions of dancers, he later departed from close observation and delighted in representing colour and shapes. His technique evolved in parallel as he relentlessly experimented with media, particularly pastel: the carefully blended single and unfixed layers of his early pastels were progressively replaced by dense accumulations of bold fluorescent cross-hatching and bright highlights.

Dancers on a Bench of around 1898 (cat. 13) is a case in point for understanding the evolution of Degas's pastel technique. While focusing on his familiar theme of dancers stretching and resting, here he builds up his composition in a series of layers of bold vertical and horizontal cross-hatching, each set with a fixative that was produced especially for him, leaving the last layer unfixed in order to achieve the brightest possible colours on the highlights. Degas liked to work quickly, but would constantly revise his compositions. Oil painting, with its long drying time, was particularly unsuited to his working habits, and he found the dry, supremely flexible medium of pastel ideal for experimenting with form and colour.

In late works such as *The Red Ballet Skirts* of around 1900 (cat. 19), Degas's dancers acquire a new monumentality, echoing the bold pastel strokes of the picture. These are no longer the graceful and svelte dancers of his earlier work; here Degas imbues his dancers with a monumental timelessness, foreshadowing some of the boldest monumental figures of Pablo Picasso (1881–1973). In these works Degas relished the opportunity to experiment with bold shapes, areas of colour and the rhythm of poses. In an act of avant-garde modernity, the medium almost becomes a subject in itself. As the poet Paul Valéry (1871–1945) observed, 'Nothing could be more modern than taking for an end what can only be a means'.[8]

Degas's friend in old age, Valéry recalled the artist's increasingly absorbing and all-consuming interest in his materials in *Degas Danse Dessin*, an insightful essay published in 1936. Valéry paints a portrait of Degas as an artist surrounded by 'bottles, flasks, pencils, bits of pastel chalk, etching needles, and all the nameless odds and ends that may come in handy one day'.[9] Degas's willingness to experiment allowed him to develop a profound and unique understanding of his materials, enabling him to transcend their limits, his use of a particular medium influencing his practice in another. This was particularly true for pastel, which became his medium of choice from around 1880. *Ballet Dancers* (cat. 14), an oil painting of around 1890–1900, was, unusually, painted on a rough unprimed canvas. The

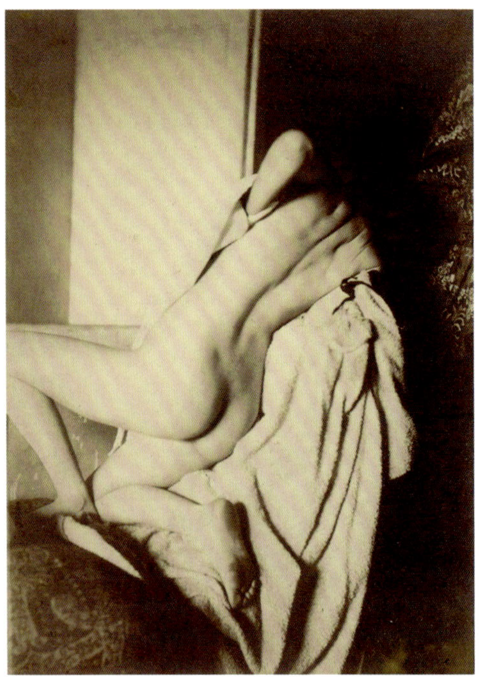

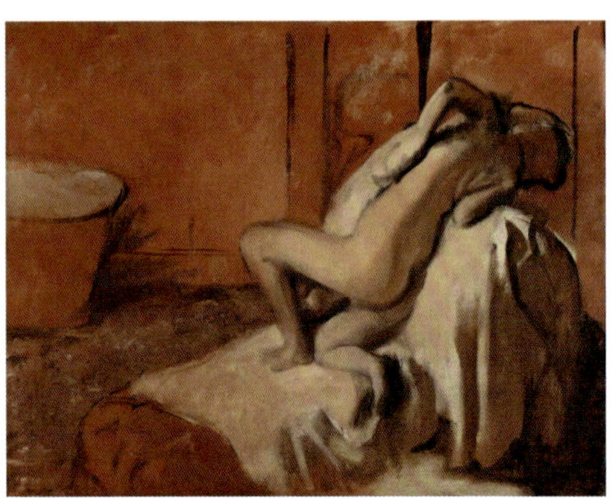

Fig. 5
Edgar Degas (1834–1917)
After the Bath, about 1896
Gelatin silver print, 16.5 × 12 cm
The J. Paul Getty Museum, Los Angeles, California
84.XM.495.2

Fig. 6
Edgar Degas (1834–1917)
After the Bath (Woman drying herself), about 1896
Oil on canvas, 89.5 × 116.8cm
Philadelphia Museum of Art, Pennsylvania
1980-6-1

coarse weave allowed Degas to paint only in short and broken brushstrokes, thus mimicking the effect obtained with pastel sticks; it also absorbed most of the oil binder of the paint, giving the work the matt, powdery texture of pastel.

He spent the last two decades of his life mostly as a recluse, depressed by his failing eyesight and alienated from his friends following his reactionary and anti-Semitic stance on the Dreyfus affair, a political scandal surrounding the case of a Jewish military officer wrongly convicted of passing military secrets to Germany. Degas spent his days repeating motifs in his studio and building a vast collection of paintings, drawings and prints: works by the great masters Ingres and Eugène Delacroix (1798–1863), but also by younger contemporary artists such as Paul Gauguin (1848–1903), whose expressive use of colour had a profound impact on him. Degas rarely exhibited or sold his work in his later years, despite his paintings having become some of the most sought-after and expensive pieces of contemporary art in the world. After 1890 only around 150 pictures, about a quarter of his output, left his studio, the rest dispersed at his death in 1917.

Alongside his unwavering fascination for dancers, from the mid-1880s Degas began depicting whole series of women bathing, washing, drying and combing their hair. Often faceless and anonymous, these women exhibit their naked bodies unselfconsciously in the privacy of their rooms, as if unaware of being observed. At a time when it was deemed improper for any man to witness such intimate moments, the works shocked and perplexed many who saw them. Who might these women be? Were they wives spied on by their unscrupulous husbands? Were they professional models demeaning themselves before the artist (a notorious bachelor), or were they prostitutes? Degas saw these works as subverting the artistic tradition of the nude, remarking: 'Up till now, the nude has always been represented in poses which presuppose an audience, but these women of mine are honest, simple folk … Here is another; she is washing her feet. It is as if you looked through a keyhole.'[10]

One of his boldest works from this last phase of his career is *Woman in a Tub* of about 1896–1901 (cat. 25). On a brilliant orange background, Degas depicts a woman bending over to pick up a fluorescent yellow sponge in the bright blue and green tub in which she is standing. The pastel is laid out quickly, in thick and bold zigzagging strokes of pure colour. Degas has mischievously found rhythm between the round tub, the roundness of the woman's buttocks and the sponge she grasps. Despite this apparent playfulness, the picture is also imbued with a certain cruelty: the figure is trapped by the tight framing of the image, incapable of standing upright. Much like the model who posed in Degas's studio, she is condemned to hold this uncomfortable position. Such painful and unnatural poses shocked and baffled viewers and critics in Degas's time, and they still do today. While some see such representations of women as misogynistic, others see these poses as an attempt to capture frank, unidealised human movements performed by ordinary women. Degas delighted in transposing these private, ephemeral moments in pastel, but as the poet and critic Stéphane Mallarmé (1842–1898) observed, Degas's bodies were mere excuses to study certain 'delicate lines and movements exquisite or grotesque', with which his art attained a 'strange new beauty'.[11]

Around 1895 Degas began experimenting with photography, producing some extraordinary works of art, character studies in light and shade, set in cavernous interiors lit by complex arrangements of artificial light sources. A gelatin silver print (fig. 5) convincingly attributed to Degas and dated about 1896, his only known photograph of a bather, allowed him to study and record a particularly difficult pose, an awkward, strained twist of the body.[12] A poignant blend of both eroticism and anguish, it is strikingly reminiscent of the contorted bodies of *Scene of War in the Middle Ages* (fig. 2) produced more than thirty years earlier. Degas worked up this composition in variants of increasing complexity (see fig. 6), culminating in *After the Bath* of about 1896 (cat. 26). The soft, muted colours and blurred contours of this oil painting seem to evoke the photograph as well as the aesthetic of pastel, highlighting the fluidity Degas was able to attain in all media. The bather's body appears almost more formless than formed, her contours dissolving into the white towel, the shadows of her spine no more defined than the patterned wallpaper beyond her or the sponge on the table. Degas's late nudes are imbued with a visceral tactility that one also finds in the wax sculptures he fashioned with his hands, which were cast in bronze after his death (see cat. 20).

As we have seen, for the best part of the 1890s Degas more or less focused exclusively – some would say obsessively – on works depicting the ballet or women at their toilette. Yet at the very end of the nineteenth century he chose to engage with a theme he had never touched upon before. His pastels of Russian – or, more accurately, Ukrainian – dancers (cats 21, 22) were as bold as the dancers themselves, their leather boots about to strike the floor rhythmically, the loops of charcoal and repeated strokes of saturated colours reflecting the frenzy of the dance.

One summer afternoon in 1899, Julie Manet (1878–1966), daughter of artist Berthe Morisot and Eugène Manet – brother of the great Edouard – found herself in a carriage, squeezed between canvases by Delacroix and their new owner, Monsieur Degas. Spotting her at an auction, the ageing artist had just invited the young Julie to his home. Degas seemed unusually jovial that day. Certainly the fact he had just bought two masterpieces at auction for 'almost nothing' must have been one reason, but something else in the air seemed to brighten his mood. The carriage pulled up in front of Degas's home, 37 rue Victor-Massé, on the lower slopes of Montmartre. In her insightful diary Julie described her encounter with Degas upstairs:

> Monsieur Degas was as kind as a sweetheart. He spoke about painting, then suddenly said to us, 'I am going to show you the orgy of colour I am making at the moment,' and then he took us up to his studio. We were very moved, because he never shows works in progress. He pulled out three pastels of women in Russian costumes with flowers in their hair, pearl necklaces, white blouses, skirts in lively hues, and red boots, dancing in an imaginary landscape, which is most real. The movements are astonishingly drawn, and the costumes are of very beautiful colours.[13]

This tale offers us a rare glimpse into Degas's studio at a time when he embarked on the last great invention of his career. He once said of himself that he would like to be 'illustrious and unknown'. He was all too successful in that aim: the personal life, thoughts and intentions of this intensely private man still elude us. His extraordinary body of work remains: complex, multifaceted and singular. Degas continually challenged himself and experimented, to the point that at his most innovative he lived in a state of almost constant dissatisfaction in his art, and consequently in himself. This was especially true as he reached the twilight of his career, prompting Camille Pissarro (1830–1903) to declare admiringly in 1898 that, unlike many others, 'Degas relentlessly moves ahead, finding expressiveness in everything that surrounds us'.[14]

NOTES

1. Vollard quoting Degas in Richard Kendall (ed.), *Degas by Himself: Drawings, Prints, Paintings, Writings*, London 1987, p. 308.
2. Degas quoting Ingres in Henri Loyrette, *Degas: The Man and his Art*, New York 1993, p. 18.
3. A virtually unknown oil study of the Spartan boys recently appeared on the art market; see Sotheby's, New York, 16 May 2017, lot 24.
4. Edmond Duranty, *La Nouvelle Peinture*, Paris 1876 (2002), p. 6.
5. For a gripping interpretation of Degas's early pictures, see Roberto Calasso, *La Folie Baudelaire*, London 2013, pp. 175–9.
6. Riopelle in David Bomford, Sarah Herring, Jo Kirby, Christopher Riopelle and Ashok Roy, *Art in the Making: Degas*, exh. cat., London 2004–5, p. 13.
7. Jill DeVonyar and Richard Kendall, *Degas and the Dance*, exh. cat., Detroit and Philadelphia 2002–3, p. 22.
8. Valéry quoted in Jodi Hauptman (ed.), *Degas: A Strange New Beauty*, exh. cat., New York 2016, p. 15.
9. Ibid., p. 13.
10. Degas quoted in George Moore, *Impressions and Opinions*, London 1891, p. 318.
11. Mallarmé's essay 'The Impressionists and Edouart Manet', reprinted in Charles S. Moffett, *The New Painting: Impressionism 1874–1886*, exh. cat., Washington and San Francisco 1986, p. 33.
12. Jean Sutherland Boggs (ed.), *Degas*, exh. cat., Paris, Ottawa and New York 1988–9, pp. 548–9.
13. Julie Manet, *Journal (1893–1899)*, Paris 1979, p. 238.
14. Janine Bailly-Herzberg (ed.), *Correspondance de Camille Pissarro*, Paris 1989, vol. 4, p. 458.

BURRELL AND DEGAS

VIVIEN HAMILTON

SIR WILLIAM BURRELL (1861–1958) was one of the great British industrialist art collectors. Beginning in the 1880s, and over seventy years, he amassed a collection of nearly nine thousand objects ranging from magnificent medieval and Renaissance tapestries, stained-glass panels and sculpture to Chinese ceramics, Islamic textiles and European paintings. The French nineteenth-century collection is renowned for its range and quality, with oils, pastels and drawings by Millet, Manet, Degas, Sisley, Gauguin and Cézanne and sculptures by Rodin.

Although wealthy, Burrell was not in the league of American art magnates such as Paul Mellon, William Randolph Hearst and J.P. Morgan, and in order to compete with them he had to use his resources carefully. On average, Burrell spent £20,000 a year until 1927, mainly on paintings. But in the following decades he spent large sums on tapestries, explaining that he was prepared to pay more for them as 'you always get your money's worth'. Indeed, in 1937 he spent more on a fifteenth-century tapestry than on either Degas's *Jockeys in the Rain* (cat. 3) or Cézanne's *Chateau de Medan*, bought the same year.

Some have accused Burrell of being too much a 'canny Scot', hunting for bargains rather than chasing masterpieces, but this Scotsman, of relatively modest means, created a collection whose stained-glass panels and tapestries rival the best examples in the Victoria and Albert Museum in London and the

Fig. 7
Sir William Burrell
(1861–1958)
Photograph, about 1906
The Burrell Collection,
Glasgow
52.29.1

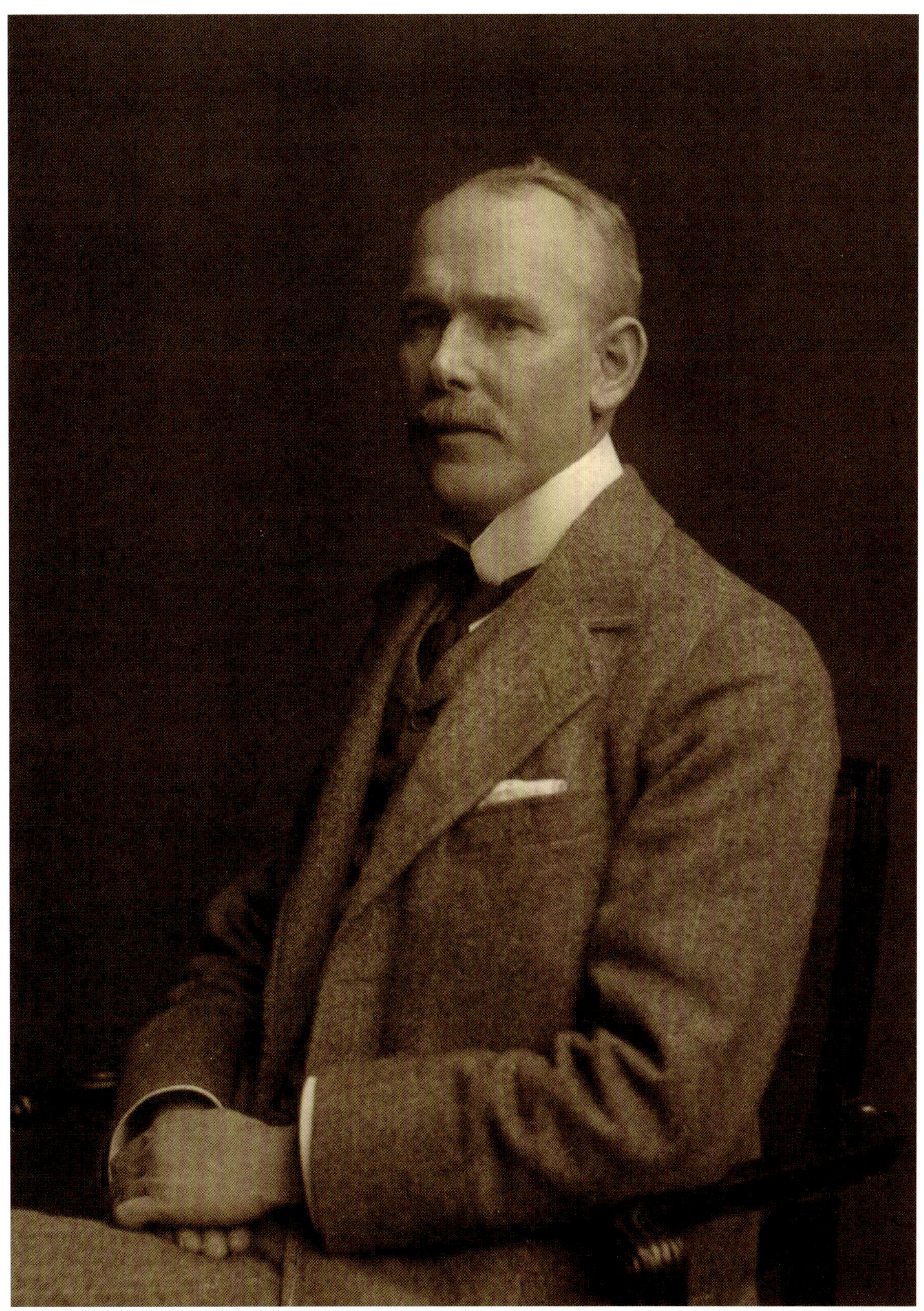

Metropolitan Museum of Art in New York. In 1944 Burrell and his wife gave the collection to Glasgow, the city of his birth and centre of his business activities, in what has been described as 'one of the greatest gifts ever made to any city in the world'.[1]

As William Wells, a former Keeper of the Burrell Collection and someone who knew the elderly Burrell, wrote,

> Burrell was of reserved character … [and] led a comparatively frugal existence … He always preserved a keen intellectual and artistic interest in his collection about which he had read widely and for the details of which he had an excellent memory. By nature he was clearly attracted by vigour of form and colour rather than by elegance.[2]

So who was this man who would not sit for a painted portrait, never recorded how or why he had amassed his wonderful collection and who proclaimed that the collection, and not the collector, was the important thing?

William Burrell was born in Glasgow in 1861 into a family that had a successful ship-owning business, with small vessels plying the canals. Glasgow by this time had grown into the second city of the British Empire. It was one of the world's great industrial cities, home to textiles, shipbuilding and heavy engineering. William Burrell joined his father in the firm in 1876 at the age of 15. His brother George specialised in the technical and engineering side of the business while William dealt with the financial and commercial aspects. After their father died in 1885 the two brothers took over and rapidly expanded the business. William had an astute commercial mind and was not afraid of taking risks. In 1894 they bought 17 ships when there was a major depression in the shipping trade. When trade picked up a few years later he sold the entire fleet. When the shipping market entered another severe depression he ordered another new fleet at rock-bottom prices. Between 1905 and 1911 he acquired a total of 32 new ships, making Burrell & Son one of the world's largest and most innovative tramp shipping companies.

During the First World War, when demand for shipping was intense, William Burrell again sold virtually the entire fleet, selling the ships for three times what they had cost new. With his share of the proceeds shrewdly invested, he devoted the remainder of his long life to what became an all-consuming passion, the amassing of a vast art collection. Burrell brought his business experience to his art collecting. He trusted art dealers because, like him, they were businessmen, but he was never keen to take the advice of art historians. With little formal learning, he acquired both his passion for art and his considerable ability as a connoisseur from extensive looking – visiting museums wherever he went, attending exhibitions and working his way round all the dealers' galleries. He was also eager to read and to learn. His own library contains plentiful evidence of his making notes in exhibition catalogues, even to the extent of compiling chronologies of Chinese dynasties, highlighting works he was interested in and adding notes of glee when he was finally able to purchase a work he desired.

We do not know when he started to collect, but it would seem that it was in the 1880s, and most likely during his many business trips to Europe. Undoubtedly a major impetus to his own collecting was the international exhibitions held in Edinburgh in 1886 and Glasgow in 1888, with their extensive sections of loans from Scottish collectors. We know that Burrell was a regular attender in 1888, even being captured in John Lavery's painting of the state opening by Queen Victoria.

He also made a series of European tours in the 1890s with his great friend the architect Robert Lorimer, when they visited the Rijksmuseum and numerous other galleries and dealers.

Glasgow was becoming increasingly important as a cultural city, with a large artistic community and art market, of which both William and his elder brother George were an enthusiastic part. George was elected a lay member of the Glasgow Art Club in November 1891, with William elected in February 1893, undoubtedly in recognition of – and to encourage – their support of contemporary artists. Similarly, both brothers subscribed to, purchased and lent to the annual exhibitions of the Royal Glasgow Institute of the Fine Arts. As a city councillor (or baillie), William was also a governor of the internationally renowned Glasgow School of Art between 1899 and 1906, although he rarely attended their meetings.

Only 13 years after the brilliantly successful 1888 exhibition, William Burrell's own importance as a collector was revealed at Glasgow's 1901 International Exhibition. With an astounding 200 objects, he was the largest single lender. His loans show the direction his collection was to take, with paintings by Manet, Géricault and Whistler, and tapestries, armour, furniture, Persian carpets and oriental ceramics.

Like many industrialists, during the 1890s Burrell purchased paintings by contemporaries or near-contemporaries rather than old masters. As he kept no inventory or documentation of any kind at this early stage, we can only build up a sense of his buying from the evidence of his loans to numerous exhibitions, including the Royal Glasgow Institute of the Fine Arts and the International Society of Sculptors, Painters and Gravers in London.

A growing market for art among the newly rich west-coast industrialists was well served by the dealers Craibe Angus, Daniel Cottier and Alexander Reid. These dealers, many with strong international connections, promoted the work of contemporary Dutch and French as well as Scottish artists. Already in the 1890s Burrell was purchasing paintings by the artists of the Hague School, including Jacob Maris (1837–1899) and his brother Matthijs (1839–1917), and by Joseph Crawhall (1861–1913), one of the Glasgow Boys, a group of Scottish artists who were reacting against the artistic establishment. Burrell also developed a taste for contemporary French art and in the 1890s was purchasing works by Honoré Daumier (1808–1879), Edouard Manet (fig. 8), Gustave Courbet (1819–1877) and Edgar Degas. His taste was shared by other local collectors, including T.G. Arthur, A.J. Kirkpatrick, William Coats and Arthur Kay. But Burrell differed from these collectors in the number of works he purchased, in the fact that his collection ranged beyond painting and because he eventually gave the collection to his native city.

In 1901 Burrell married Constance Mitchell and bought their elegant marital home at 8 Great Western Terrace in Glasgow's fashionable West End. Here they lived surrounded by treasures including tapestries, stained glass, wood carvings, alabaster, glass, furniture and paintings. As his collecting career evolved and matured, his growing interest in medieval art prompted him to buy Hutton Castle in the Scottish Borders in 1916, which spurred him to collect even more in this area. When Burrell moved to Hutton Castle in 1927, after it had undergone extensive refurbishment, his nineteenth-century French and Dutch paintings did not move with him, as they were already on loan to major museums throughout Britain.

As his stature and reputation as a collector grew, Burrell gained influence by becoming a trustee, first of the National Galleries of Scotland in 1923 and then in

Fig. 8
Edouard Manet (1832–1883)
Women drinking Beer, 1878
Pastel on primed linen canvas, 61 × 50.8 cm
The Burrell Collection, Glasgow
35.305

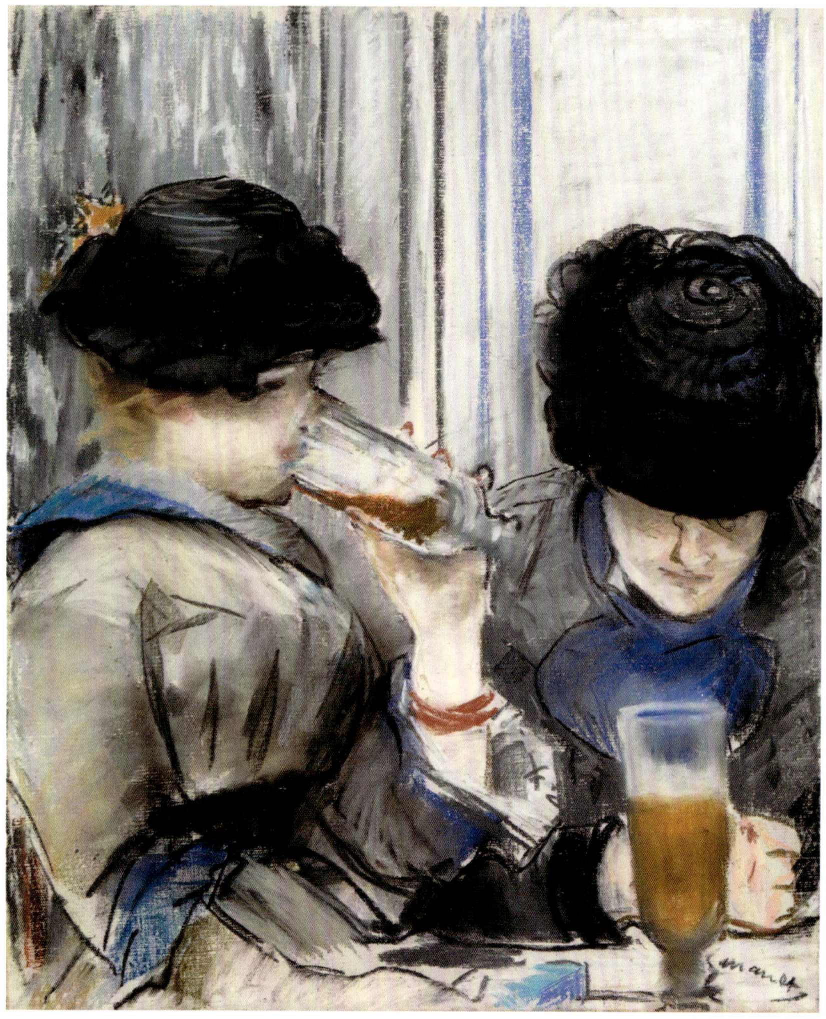

1927 of the National Gallery of British Art (now Tate Britain). In 1927 he was knighted for his services to art. Having all but retired from the shipping business, Burrell focused the rest of his life on developing the collection. He managed his money carefully and was largely unaffected by the financial turbulence of the 1930s.

As well as lending works, Burrell donated a number of items to museums in the 1920s, including 48 paintings and drawings to Glasgow in 1924. In the 1930s he formed the idea of creating a permanent collection to be handed over to public ownership. He had discussions with a number of interested parties before finally settling on Glasgow in 1944, which crucially agreed to accept and keep the collection in its entirety. By this time it numbered some six thousand items. But his taste for new acquisitions remained undiminished and the collection now grew at an even faster rate: between 1944 and 1957 a further two thousand items were added to the original gift. In these last years he continued to buy in the same fields as before, but concentrated on certain areas that he considered needed strengthening. During this time he contacted the Glasgow museum staff on an almost daily basis and these letters reveal the care he felt for his objects and his desire to communicate that love and knowledge both to the museum staff and to the local public.

COLLECTING DEGAS

In 1949, when asked about Degas, Burrell wrote: '… I am very sorry I never met him. Reid might have taken me to his studios had we been in Paris together but I was hardly ever in Paris at the same time as Reid.'[3]

Burrell had a particular passion for the work of Edgar Degas and over a period of 40 years he purchased 23 oils, pastels and drawings from dealers in Glasgow, London, Paris and Switzerland. They range from early oils to late and magnificent pastels covering the artist's favoured subjects of dancers, horses, modern life and women bathing. He gave one pastel, *Russian Dancers* (cat. 21), to the town of Berwick-upon-Tweed, but the rest of the works form part of the Burrell Collection in Glasgow. Burrell's reasons for collecting works by Degas do not survive in the written record; he never recorded why he collected them or what he thought of them. From 1911 he kept purchase books to document his acquisitions, but they provide no clues as to his motives. He never seems to have lived with his Degas pictures, as they were somewhat alien to the medieval aesthetic with which he surrounded himself, but instead preferred to lend them to museums and galleries.

Works by Degas were in London collections as early as the 1870s and could be seen, and were frequently reviewed, in exhibitions throughout the 1880s and 1890s. But how and what might William Burrell have seen by the contemporary French artist in this period? It may have been Glasgow's International Exhibition in 1888 that brought Degas to his attention for the first time. Included in the exhibition was *Rehearsal Hall at the Opéra, rue Le Peletier* of 1872 (Musée d'Orsay, Paris). This had been lent by the English merchant banker Louis Huth, who had bought it earlier that year, making him the first British collector to purchase a work by Degas.

There is another intriguing possibility that needs further research. Sir Peter Coats, the leading thread manufacturer, philanthropist and art collector, acquired three works by Degas in 1885, including the glorious 1883 pastel *Ballet Dancers on the Stage* (fig. 9). These were the first works by Degas in Scotland, and it is possible that Burrell saw or heard about them. Even if he did not, he most certainly did see works by Degas at La Société des Beaux-Arts, the Glasgow gallery of the enterprising and dynamic dealer Alex Reid. Reid had spent nearly two years working in Paris with Theo van Gogh (1857–1891) in the Montmartre gallery of Boussod and Valadon. Reid and the two Van Gogh brothers, Theo and Vincent (1853–1890), even shared an apartment in the rue Lepic. Through Theo, Reid had the chance to see works by Manet, Sisley and Pissarro and had an entrée to the studios of many of the French Impressionist artists, including Edgar Degas, with whom Theo was on friendly terms. Indeed, in January 1888 Theo had Degas's pastels of women washing on display.

In late 1891 Reid held an exhibition entitled *A Small Collection of Pictures by Degas and Others* with Arthur Collie of 39b Old Bond Street. Although no works were bought from the London show, when the exhibition moved to Reid's own gallery in Glasgow in February 1892 he sold three pictures by Degas to two Glasgow collectors. T.G. Arthur purchased Degas's pastel *At the Milliner's* of 1882 (Metropolitan Museum of Art, New York) for £800. His business partner, Arthur Kay, bought the brilliantly contemporary and daring oil *In a Café (L'Absinthe)* of 1875–6 (Musée d'Orsay, Paris), which Reid had just purchased at auction in London for £180. Kay, unsure of his purchase, returned it immediately, but then

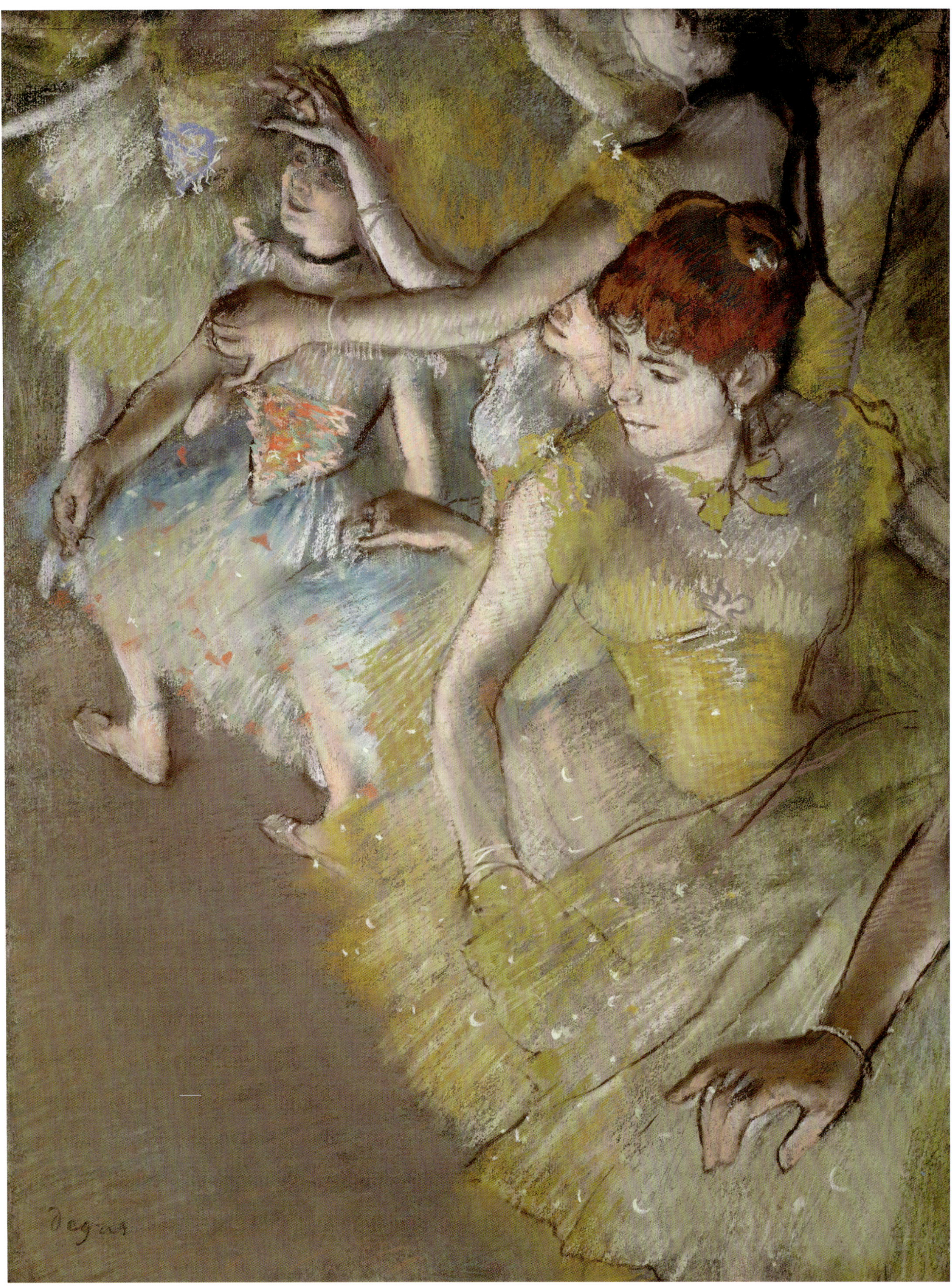
degas

went back to Reid once more and not only bought the painting for a second time but also purchased the pastel *Dancers in the Rehearsal Room with a Double Bass* of about 1882–5 (Metropolitan Museum of Art, New York). Kay lent both works to the Grafton Gallery in February 1893, only to sell them a few months later. More a collector of old masters, he was undoubtedly perplexed by the running battle waged in newspaper columns about his ownership of *L'Absinthe*, one writer questioning how he could live with a picture of 'human degradation'. In a letter of 29 March 1893 to the *Westminster Gazette* he predicted: 'Corot and Millet suffered at the hands of the critic; now they are understood. Degas will be understood, and in a few years those who blame will praise, and those who curse will bless.'

An intriguing and unsolved puzzle is whether Burrell owned Degas's *Première Danseuse (The Encore)* (fig. 10) as a result of Reid's 1891 exhibition, where 'Une danseuse' is listed as no. 17 in the catalogue. The pastel was illustrated in an article on Degas by Theodore Duret in the 1894 *Art Journal* and is credited to the collection of William Burrell of Glasgow. Was the scandal of Kay's purchase of *L'Absinthe* the reason why, if he did indeed own it, Burrell returned the work to Reid, who then sent it to the Galerie Camentron et Martin, as he had done with other works by the artist?

William's brother George was also an early purchaser of Degas. In 1895 he lent 'The Ballet' to the Royal Glasgow Institute of the Fine Arts, of which the *Scotsman* observed that 'the type of women selected for representation is by no means attractive'. In 1913 George Burrell lent 'Ballet Girl' to the Royal Scottish Academy and in 1923 he lent 'Dancing Girls' to the Paisley Art Institute exhibition. However, given the vagaries of naming paintings, it is possible that these are all the same work.

While more research may establish with greater certainty the identity of Burrell's first work by Degas, we do know that the tiny oil sketch *Woman looking through Field Glasses* (cat. 1) was definitely in his collection by 1902. This early purchase is also one of the most revealing and fascinating. While Burrell may have bought it because of its subject, a figural composition and of horseracing, or because of its small scale and probably correspondingly small price, it sums up the essence of Degas's art and Burrell's collecting. Fundamentally, this work challenges the viewer to consider the importance of looking. This was the first of the 22 works by Degas that William Burrell acquired and that are still in the Collection. He probably bought it from Alex Reid around the turn of the century but then had a change of heart, as he included it in one of the auctions of works from his collection held at Christie's, London, in May and June 1902. The sale included works by Dutch and French nineteenth-century artists, including Maris, Monticelli and Manet. Most of the paintings failed to find a purchaser. Burrell's reason for selling is not known but may have been prompted by his recent marriage and move to his Great Western Terrace home with its 'Gothic' interior. A need for funds may also have prompted the sale, as Burrell and his brother George sought to raise capital for the new fleet they were planning. Writing 40 years later about the Monticelli he had sold and then repurchased, Burrell did confirm that shortage of cash was a motive: 'I had to sell'.

As there is no written evidence of Burrell's acquisition of *Woman looking through Field Glasses*, we do not know if he was aware of its provenance, something that he tended to include in his purchase book entries. The back of the canvas is inscribed in Degas's own writing 'vers 1865' (see. p. 44). Devastated by the sudden death of his writer friend Edmond Duranty, Degas included the picture in an auction sale in aid of Duranty's widow in January 1881.

OPPOSITE Fig. 9
Edgar Degas (1834–1917)
Ballet Dancers on the Stage, 1883
Pastel on paper, 61.6 × 47.3 cm
Dallas Museum of Art, Texas
1986.277

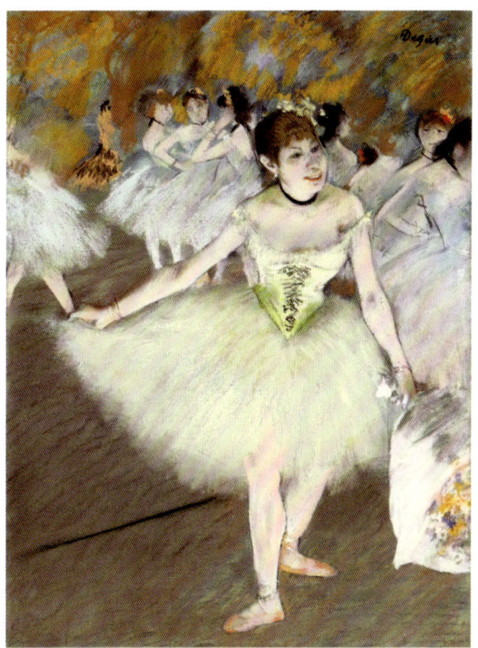

Fig. 10
Edgar Degas (1834–1917)
Premier Danseuse (The Encore), 1879–81
Pastel on paper, 58.5 × 44.8 cm
Private collection, Europe

Burrell's next purchase, in December 1917, was of a strong and daring late pastel, *Three Dancers* of about 1900 – 5 (cat. 17), with its vibrant colours and aggressively jagged shadows. Was Burrell inspired not so much by the recent death of Degas a few months earlier as by the countless articles and laudatory obituaries then devoted to the artist? This work has a wonderful provenance that can be traced all the way back to Degas. It belonged to Marczell de Nemes, Hungarian financier, art dealer and collector from Budapest, and was sold from his collection in June 1913 by the Galerie Manzi Joyant in Paris, from where it was bought by Alex Reid for £660. Reid lent the pastel immediately to the Royal Glasgow Institute of the Fine Arts, where Burrell could have seen it. Believing that the pastel was of museum quality, Reid then sent it to the Scottish National Gallery on approval, at a cost of £670, but it was returned. When Burrell bought it in 1917 he secured a bargain, paying only £650.

Degas cared passionately about how his works were framed and designed frames that he considered suitable. Over time frames are often changed, either by a new owner or by a dealer; one of the things that makes *Three Dancers* so special is that it remains in Degas's own frame.

Burrell acquired his next work by Degas from Reid six years later, doubtless motivated by the exhibition *Masterpieces of French Art* that Reid held in his London premises in collaboration with Thomas Agnew. Burrell bought *Preparation for the Class* (cat. 12) on 15 June 1923, for which he was prepared to pay the hefty sum (for him) of £2,500. Reid had purchased it only a few weeks earlier from the Parisian dealer Paul Rosenberg and within days had sold it Burrell. But unlike *Three Dancers,* with its magnificent original frame, this beautiful pastel had an unattractive modern one. Research revealed the type of frame that had been on the work when it was in Rosenberg's hands, and Glasgow Museums has now purchased an appropriate period frame.

Some five months later, in November 1923, Burrell bought two important pastels from Lefevre's London exhibition *The Impressionist School and some Great French Painters of the Nineteenth Century*. Alex Reid's son, A.J. McNeill Reid, recounted how, in 1922, he had seen *Portrait of Edmond Duranty* (cat. 2) in the window of the Galerie Barbazanges in Paris. The asking price was £1,100. Armed with a photograph, he returned to Glasgow to ask for his father's approval to buy it. Alex Reid was against the purchase, saying that it would be difficult to sell if Burrell did not want it. McNeill Reid cancelled his deal. A few months later Lefevre bought it and included it in his exhibition. Reid should not have been so nervous, as Burrell duly paid £1,900 for the portrait and also acquired *At the Jeweller's* (cat. 10) for £625 at the same time. Not long afterwards Reid and Lefevre joined forces, providing Reid with a London gallery.

In April 1924 William Burrell lent part of his collection, including six works by Degas, to the National Gallery, Millbank (now Tate). The Gallery's trustees had accepted the loan of Burrell's collection 'with a view to increasing the interest in the collection of Modern Foreign Art, which will shortly be housed in the new Gallery now being built on the vacant site behind the Gallery at Millbank'.[4] This exhibition of his private collection in the nation's capital was a great honour for Burrell. Not only was his collection being given a national stamp of approval, it was being used to develop public taste and indicate the Gallery's future intentions as to the formation and display of a modern collection. The loan exhibition was reviewed by the artist and critic Walter Sickert (1860–1942), who hinted that Burrell's collection was too conservative and its quality dubious: 'Purchases or gifts to museums of modern painting, like the one at Millbank, should perhaps, though this is a matter of opinion, observe two rules. They should aim at the best available example of each painter. They would probably do well to limit themselves to one example.' He also wrote: 'Important [works by] Degas that might easily have been bought in the period over which this collection extends have long been safely housed elsewhere.'[5]

We must surely take issue with Sickert's assessment of Burrell's works by Degas. The challenge is in the use of the adjective 'important' and the implication that Burrell, while having the opportunity to buy major works, never chose to exercise it. Of the six works by Degas included in the 1924 exhibition, there can be no doubting the significance of the *Portrait of Edmond Duranty*. This magnificent picture, of Degas's friend, the novelist and critic, had been shown in two of the Impressionist exhibitions, the Fourth Exhibition in 1879 and the Fifth in 1880 (after Duranty's sudden death). Today Duranty's reputation rests on his essay *La Nouvelle Peinture* (*The New Painting*), published in 1876, in which he discussed the evolution of a new stylistic approach to painting but deliberately avoided the use of the term Impressionism. Many of Duranty's ideas were close to those shared by Degas, and for a time some people even believed that it had been Degas and not Duranty who had written it. Degas's portrait of Duranty perfectly sums up the guiding principles of 'the new painting' as expounded in Duranty's essay. Duranty had challenged his artist friends to paint the world around them and to capture the telling gesture, a challenge to which Degas responded in this very portrait. There can be no doubting the sitter's profession – he is surrounded by books, manuscripts and ink bottles – or the serious nature of his task, his fingers pointing to his head. But this is certainly not an easy picture and it remained unsold at the artist's death. Throughout the period 1923–4 it appeared in many dealers' exhibitions and Burrell would have had numerous opportunities to see it before deciding to buy it.

Burrell had acquired four works by Degas in the months leading up to the Millbank show. The prospect of having his collection exhibited in the capital may have acted as an incentive to his purchasing. The four works included the small and delicate *Green Ballet Skirt* (cat. 18) and a large and beautiful rehearsal scene, *Preparation for the Class* (cat. 12). That Burrell admired Degas's scenes of the ballet is not in doubt: today nine of the 22 works in the collection are of ballet dancers. Burrell must have had an interest in the subject but, like Degas, he also loved line and colour, and the medium of pastel. While it is possible that Burrell preferred pastels because they were usually less expensive than oils, the particular works he chose were often costly. *Preparation for the Class*, for example, cost him £2,500. If Burrell felt that Sickert was right in saying that the best works by Degas were 'safely housed elsewhere', then he could still seek such works out.

The Rehearsal (cat. 11) was purchased by Theo van Gogh, of the Boussod and Valadon gallery, from the Parisian dealer Georges Petit for 5,220 French francs on 12 October 1888. Only a few weeks later, on 29 November, Theo sold the painting to the French artist Jacques-Emile Blanche (1861–1942) for 8,000 French francs. In May 1926 it was bought by McNeill Reid, from whom Burrell then purchased it a few weeks later for £6,500.

A year later Burrell bought the small oil *In the Tuileries Gardens* (cat. 7) from Reid & Lefevre for £1,600. Painted about 1880, Degas had either sold or given the painting to his friend and publisher Michel Manzi. The Italian-born Manzi, like Theo van Gogh, worked for Boussod and Valadon.

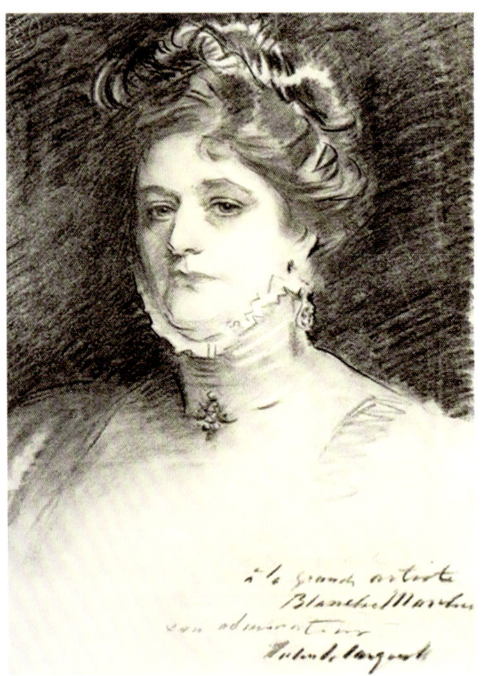

Fig. 11
John Singer Sargent (1856–1925)
Portrait of Blanche Marchesi, 1910
Black chalk on paper, 63 x 48 cm
Private collection

Burrell's last major purchase, also bought through Reid & Lefevre, was *Jockeys in the Rain* (cat. 3), which he bought in May 1937 for £3,885 plus commission. This magnificent pastel had belonged to another Scottish collector, Leonard Gow, who had bought it from Lefevre's 1928 exhibition. Like Burrell, Gow was involved in the shipping industry and shared Burrell's passion for oriental ceramics and for the works of Joseph Crawhall. The former Director of Glasgow Museums T.J. Honeyman, who knew Burrell well, recorded in his autobiography that 'I think Sir William Burrell had missed getting it earlier. He once said to me "It's no use being an 'also ran' in the Art Race. You have to be first".'[6]

From the early 1920s Burrell also bought from dealers in Paris, in particular Georges Bernheim, from whom he purchased three wonderful pastels. The astonishing *Red Ballet Skirts* (cat. 19) cost £434 in October 1921, only three years or so after it had been sold from Degas's studio for 16,000 French francs. In 1927 Burrell bought *Laundresses* (cat. 9) and then in 1933 *Women in a Theatre Box* (cat. 23), each for £1,000. When Burrell noted this last acquisition in his purchase book he later added the relevant Degas sale information, having by this time bought his own volumes of the catalogue.

Until the early 1920s Burrell had largely chosen to purchase strong late works, especially pastels, but he then expanded the scope of his collecting to include smaller pastels and also drawings. Was this because he wanted his collection to give a more rounded view of the artist or was it because of their lower prices? In late 1922 he purchased the *Dancer at the Barre* (cat. 15) from J. Allard for only £28 11s. 5d. The work is inscribed, though today the inscription is almost illegible. Was Burrell aware that Degas had given this small drawing to the arts journalist Louis de Fourcaud (about 1851–1914)? If he had he would have been delighted, as Fourcaud had written one of the first books on one of Burrell's favourite artists, Théodule Ribot (1839–1916), and had known both Eugène Boudin (1824–1898) and Henri Fantin-Latour (1836–1904) well, whom Burrell also collected. Another inexpensive drawing, also from Allard, was *After the Bath* (cat. 28), which Burrell bought in April 1923 for £14.

A further interesting purchase, possibly inspired by seeing it in an exhibition, was *The Green Ballet Skirt* (cat. 18), which Burrell bought from Knoedler in October 1923 for £500.This graceful and fresh pastel had been purchased from Degas by Durand-Ruel in May 1898. It was exhibited in Durand-Ruel's major London exhibition in the Grafton Galleries in early 1905. By 1910 it was owned by Blanche Marchesi (1863–1940; fig. 11), the world-famous mezzo-soprano and voice teacher. From exhibition catalogues we know that Blanche owned a number of works by Degas. A keen supporter of Impressionist art, she 'generously and enthusiastically' organised a Sunday evening concert in 1905 in aid of a 'French Impressionist Fund' set up by the critic Frank Rutter to help with purchases of art for the national collections.

Burrell bought another pastel, *Russian Dancers* (cat. 21), from Allard in December 1929 for £144. Another dealer from whom he purchased many works, usually drawings and sometimes of lesser quality, was the Scottish-born David Croal Thomson, whose London gallery was called Barbizon House. Here Burrell bought *Woman combing Her Hair* (cat. 30) in April 1924 for £100 and three years later, for £130, the wonderful *Dancer adjusting her Shoulder Strap* (cat. 29), which he may have seen in the Leicester Gallery Degas exhibition in 1922. And he purchased the drawing *The End of the Race* (cat. 4) in 1930 for £70, perhaps both for the subject and the price.

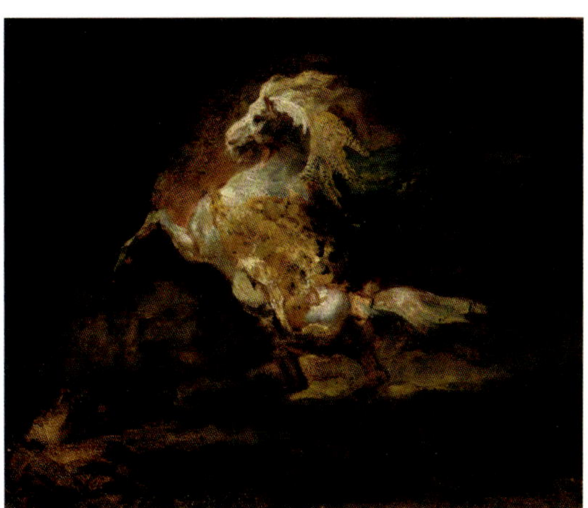

Fig. 12
Théodore Géricault (1791–1824)
A Prancing Grey Horse, 1812
Oil on canvas, 45.1 × 54.6 cm
The Burrell Collection, Glasgow
35.271

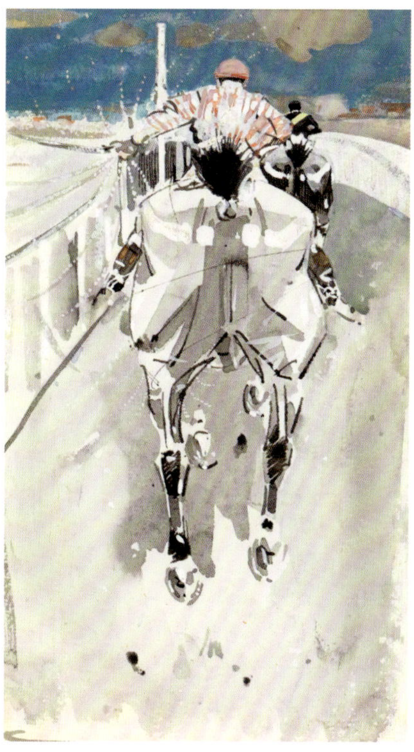

Fig. 13
Joseph Crawhall (1861–1913)
The Race, about 1890
Watercolour heightened with bodycolour on paper, 23.2 × 14.2 cm
The Burrell Collection, Glasgow
35.180

He continued to buy works by Degas into the 1930s, turning to the Lausanne-based dealer Paul Vallotton in July 1933 for *Woman in a Tub* (cat. 25), for which he paid £360. Four years later he purchased *Woman in a Tub* (cat. 24) from Mouradian and Vallotton on 2 August 1937 for £186 1s. 11d. This dark and difficult pastel had been in Agnews' Degas exhibition in 1936 and then in the 1937 Adams Gallery Degas show, but Burrell had not been tempted. The pastel was one that Degas had exhibited at the Eighth Impressionist exhibition in 1886.

The last works by Degas that Burrell added to his collection were another two he bought from Adams in 1937, which had been exhibited earlier that year: *Woman at her Toilette* (cat. 32) and *Horse tied to a Tree* (cat. 6). The only possible reason for the addition of this slight work is Burrell's love of horses. These feature heavily elsewhere in his collection in tapestries, stained glass and ceramics, as well as in the wonderful paintings by Théodore Géricault and Joseph Crawhall (figs 12, 13).

Two years after giving his collection to the City of Glasgow, Burrell decided that several works should be removed and donated instead to the gallery in Berwick-upon-Tweed, close to his Hutton Castle home. Among the works included was *Russian Dancers* (cat. 21). T.J. Honeyman wrote to Burrell pleading against this gift:

> With regard to the Degas, I am in the course of preparing an article 'Degas in the Burrell Collection', and a featured point in that article will be the extraordinary range of Degas of different kinds, one way or another, assembled by one collector in his lifetime. Even the removal of a sketch from this group weakens the argument. On the level of scholarship it is of infinitely greater value to keep these pictures together than to have one isolated at Berwick. To sum up and with the utmost respect I do insist that the removal of these … particular items weakens the Burrell Collection … and I very seriously ask you to reconsider again these two items.[6]

Burrell was not prepared to budge, replying: 'The Degas is only a sketch and you have … the best picture he ever painted…' (the latter was not specified, but is perhaps *The Rehearsal*, cat. 11).[8] Honeyman had to give up and his article in the *Glasgow Art Review* duly appeared in 1946 without *Russian Dancers*. Despite the loss of this work, Burrell's collection in Glasgow remains one of the largest and most significant holdings of Degas in the UK. Its range is truly impressive and there are a number of individual masterpieces, including, as Burrell said, the best picture Degas ever painted.

NOTES

1 John Julius Norwich, introduction to *The Burrell Collection*, London and Glasgow 1983.
2 William Wells, 'Sir William Burrell', in *Treasures from the Burrell Collection*, exh. cat., London 1975, p. 11.
3 Letter to A.J. McNeil Reid, National Library of Scotland, Special Collections, Acc. 6925.
4 From the 'Introduction' in the exhibition handlist (*Loan Exhibition of the Burrell Collection, National Gallery, Millbank*, London 1924).
5 Walter Sickert, 'Mr Burrell's collection at the Tate', *Southport Visitor*, 5 and 19 April 1924.
6 T.J. Honeyman, *Art and Audacity*, London 1971, p. 139.
7 T.J. Honeyman to Sir William Burrell, letter of 7 March 1949 in the Burrell archive, Glasgow Museums Resource Centre (GMA.2013.1.2.16.188).
8 Sir William Burrell to T.J. Honeyman, letter of 9 March 1949 in the Burrell archive, Glasgow Museums Resource Centre (GMA.2013.1.2.16.189).

A PRACTISED TOUCH: EDGAR DEGAS AND THE ART OF PASTEL

HARRIET K. STRATIS

SIR WILLIAM BURRELL acquired art and artefacts from all corners of the world, to amass a formidable collection. In some areas he collected extensively, while in others he obtained a few select works. He was perhaps best known for his holdings of medieval stained glass, Chinese ceramics and bronzes, Gothic wood and stone sculptures, as well as Egyptian and Islamic artefacts, and these treasures could not be more different from the works of the French Impressionists that he collected concurrently. Among them, surprisingly, is a significant gathering of works on paper by Edgar Degas. From intimate charcoal drawings to monumental pastel compositions, these works are as delicate as their antecedents in the collection are robust. Perhaps the vibrant pastel powders that Degas had drawn on paper were as alluring to Burrell as the brilliant colours of light that passed through the collector's panes of stained glass. Burrell acquired pastels that reveal Degas's nuanced achievements using the medium over a period of three decades that extended from the late 1870s

Detail of cat. 12

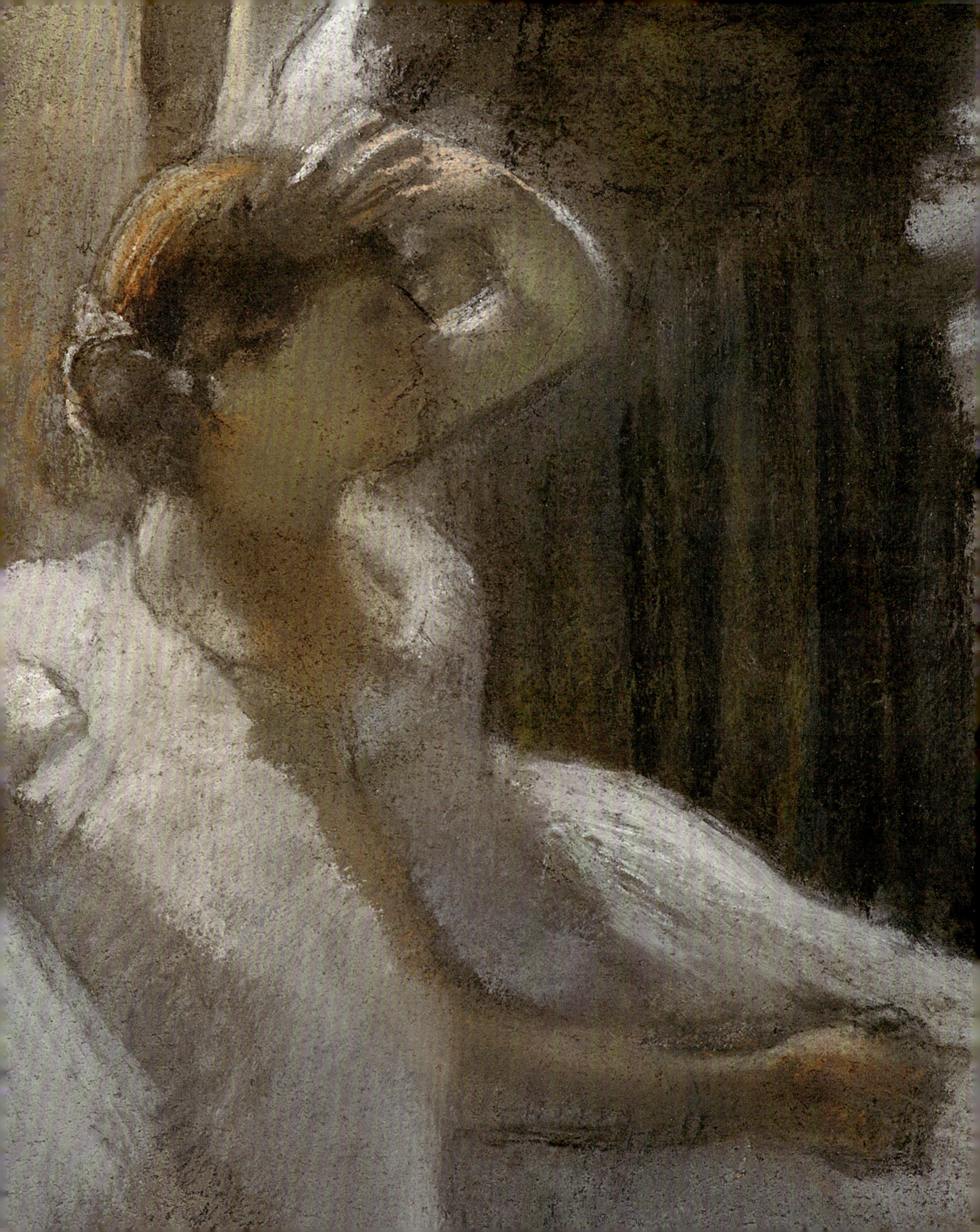

up to and beyond 1900. These works reveal Degas to be a consummate draughtsman who used pastel to augment emphatic charcoal lines with bursts of colour. They also show him to be a colourist who, when applying the medium more thickly in broad swathes, could subsume any visual evidence of charcoal under strata of brightly coloured pastel.

Degas's methods and materials changed significantly over a 25-year period and reflect, in part, a growing appreciation for spontaneity that was popular among French artists in the last two decades of the nineteenth century. Acceptable subject matter was changing too, and Degas took inspiration from the figures he encountered on the stage, at the racetrack, in the brothels and café-concerts, and even within the hot, steamy confines of the laundresses' shops. Pastel is a medium that is well suited to capturing the moment: sticks of pastel are portable, available in various sizes and shapes, and in myriad colours made all the more vibrant by the introduction of aniline dyes into the manufacturing process during the latter half of the nineteenth century. The sticks were manufactured in different densities depending on the types and amounts of binders and fillers added to their raw pigments. Common binders included gums that, when mixed with powdered pigments and fillers like kaolin, made the sticks very hard so that fine, compact lines could be drawn with them. Soft sticks made with minimal amounts of binder and fillers held the pastel particles more loosely, so that when drawing with them, the colours were dispersed into broad, powdery strokes.[1]

Artists' papers in a greater array of textures and sizes were also being developed specifically for pastellists. These too became available in a spectrum of aniline-dyed colours that would complement the tones and physical characteristics of pastel and charcoal. Degas selected pink, green, orange and blue papers of the brightest hues for his charcoal renderings as early as the 1870s. Some papers were manufactured with sandpaper-like coatings onto which pastel particles could cling; others had very fibrous, toothy surfaces that captured and held the particles of powdery media. Degas worked in pastel on both types, often using the tip of a finger or a leather stump to blend or 'sweeten' the pastel into the papers' surfaces. Another liberating innovation, paper sold on rolls rather than in standard-sized sheets, afforded artists the opportunity to create ever-larger compositions. Degas purchased rolls of tracing paper and produced a number of extraordinary pastels and charcoal drawings in series throughout the 1890s, exploiting the translucency of the tracing paper to copy, invert and reuse forms.[2] As the products of the industrial revolution helped to flood the art market with new materials, Degas eagerly took them to hand and quickly embraced them.

Unlike working with oil paints, which must dry for a considerable period of time between applications, drawing with pastels on paper is an immediate process. However, pastel can be a difficult medium to master. When drawn onto paper in a single layer, care is required so that individual strokes remain distinct; in multiple layers, a delicate touch must be exerted to assure that colours are not over-blended and muddied into one another. Degas's earliest forays into drawing with pastels in the late 1860s and early 1870s are astonishingly accomplished. His production reflects a deep understanding of eighteenth-century precedents in which the medium was primarily applied to fibrous papers in a single layer; additional layers of pastel were used sparingly for highlights and added details; only the most delicate stumping was used to blend tones; and more rarely, wire brushes or combs were drawn

Fig. 14
Maurice Quentin de la Tour (1704–1788)
Self-portrait in a Bullseye Window, about 1737
Pastel on grey paper, 61.5 × 48.5 cm
Graphic Arts Cabinet of the Museums of Art and History, Geneva, Legacy Edouard Sarasin
1917-0027

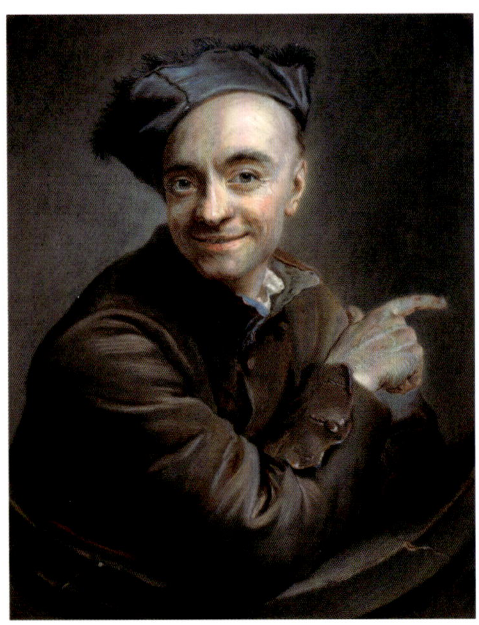

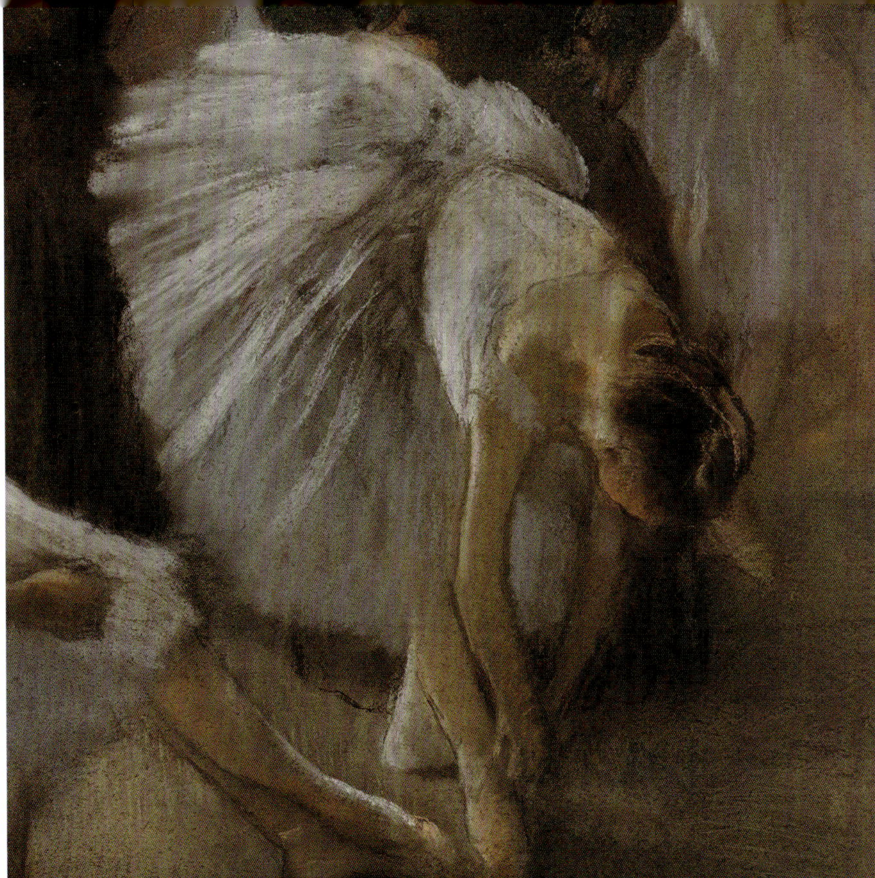

Detail of cat. 12

through the media to impart finely incised parallel lines into selected passages (fig. 14). Like the eighteenth-century pastellists he wished to emulate, Degas used little or no fixative (a spray- or brush-applied adhesive) in his earliest pastels to secure the powdery media to the paper.

Many aspects of eighteenth-century pastel technique can be ascribed to Degas's *Preparation for the Class* (cat. 12; see detail p. 33), from the nature of the paper he used, to the application of the media, to the absence of fixative. Degas also looked to the painting techniques of early Italian Renaissance masters, in which green underpaint was prevalent in the flesh tones.[3] Re-purposing the method, green undertones are often visible in his early pastels as a means to impart shading, as, for example, in the face and arm of the seated dancer in *Preparation for the Class*. Blended undertones are visible throughout the drawing. The pastel colours are well worked into the surface of the fibrous paper with stump, rag, fingertips and side of the palm. Strokes of soft white pastel dissolve into powders as they are blended into diaphanous folds of fabric. Over these, delicate unblended strokes of harder, brighter pastel colours are applied to signify the light falling on to the floor from the window at left, and on to the highpoints of the ruffled tulle of the dancers' skirts (see detail, above). Pastel applications conceal the presence of an underlying charcoal drawing that is only visible under magnification.

However, an unfinished pastel from around the same period, *At the Jeweller's* (cat. 10), does provide a glimpse into this consistent step in Degas's working process, an important one in which he used charcoal to sketch underdrawings before proceeding to work in pastel.[4] At the far right of this composition, Degas wiped pastel away from the proper left side of the figure in the foreground to expose charcoal lines initially drawn to summarily sketch a third figure. He used yellow

Detail of cat. 10

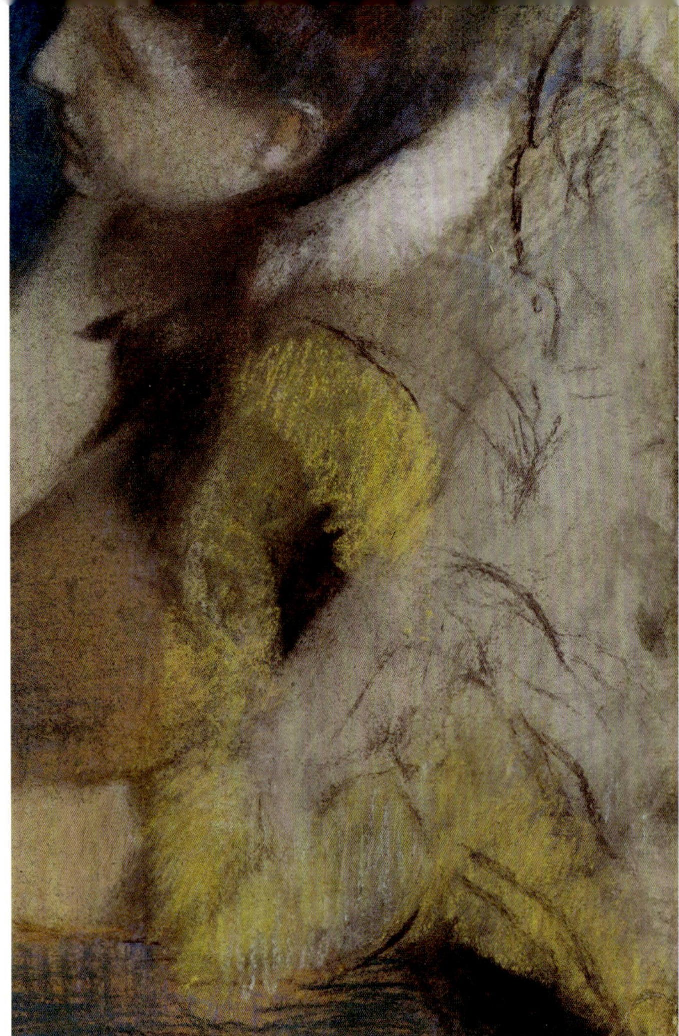

and black pastel to re-establish the placement of a bent right arm and limp wrist, and a partially extended left hand (see detail, above). To modify the narrative further, Degas faintly indicated a jewel on a chain extending from the figure's downturned wrist. It is here that the artist abandoned the composition despite the degree of finish he had attained in the rest of the sheet, perhaps unable to reconcile the perspective required to articulate fully the third figure in the limited space remaining in the lower right.

For his pastel *Laundresses* (about 1882–4; cat. 9) Degas selected a dark pink sheet, which has altered to light brown owing to the fading of an aniline dye component in the paper.[5] To the sheet he applied several lightly fixed layers of pastel, applying his strokes in a series of distinct hatch marks. He spray-applied a fixative that has selectively darkened over time so that, upon close inspection, a series of faint spatter marks are now visible. However, he left the uppermost passages of white and golden yellow pastel unfixed, for example where he added a single delicate golden stroke to place a ring on the finger of the standing laundress.

Further into the 1880s Degas used fixatives more liberally to secure his layers of pastel to paper, and as his proficiency with this material increased, he used it to achieve new aesthetic ends in larger, more ambitious compositions.[6] In one such drawing, *Jockeys in the Rain* (about 1883–6; cat. 3), the artist masterfully alternated layers of pastel with spray-applied fixative to transform a soft, powdery matt surface into one that was harder and more resilient and glistened when viewed at an angle. On to this hard, compacted, colourful base Degas added more pastel, free of the risk

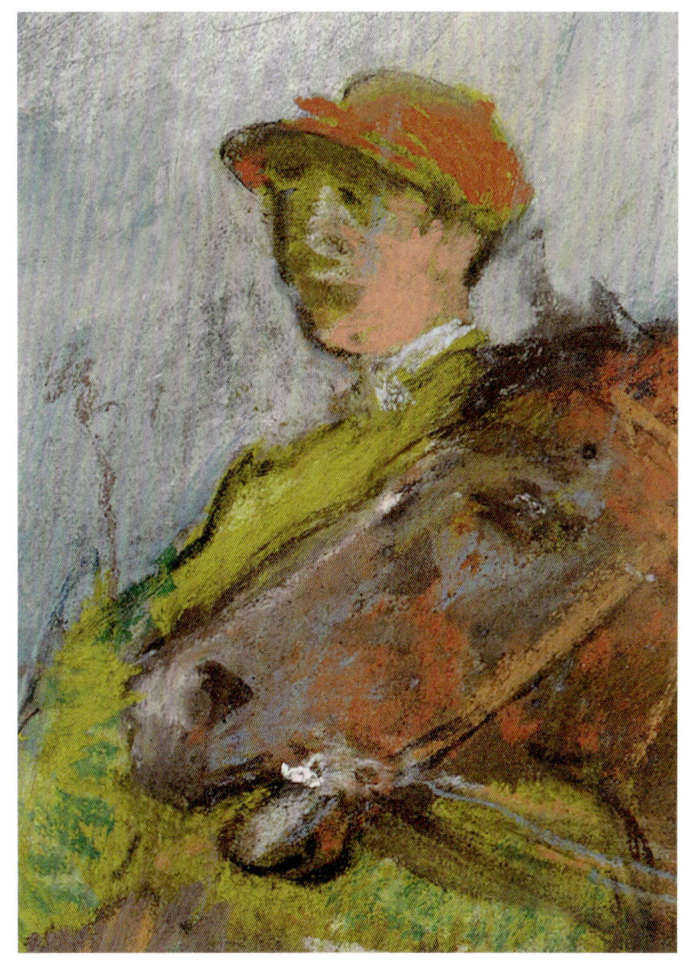

Details of cat. 3

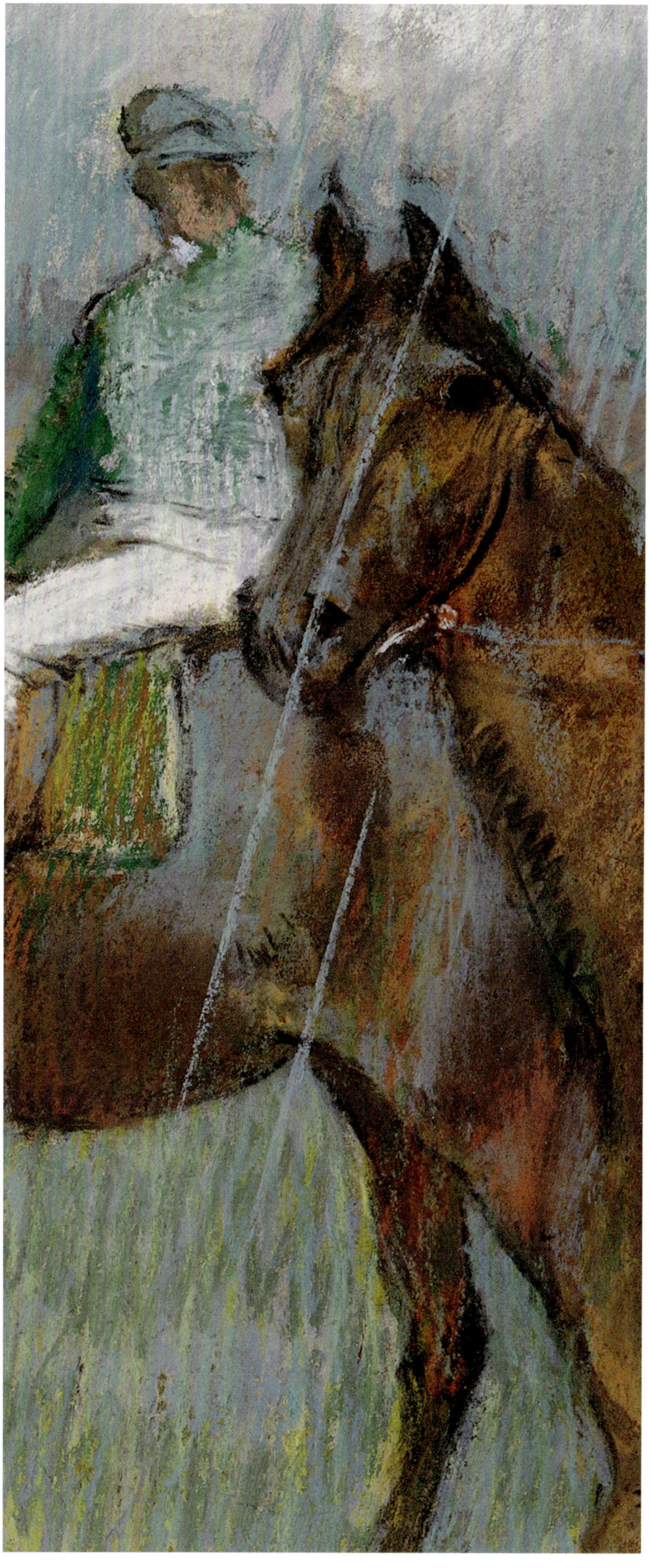

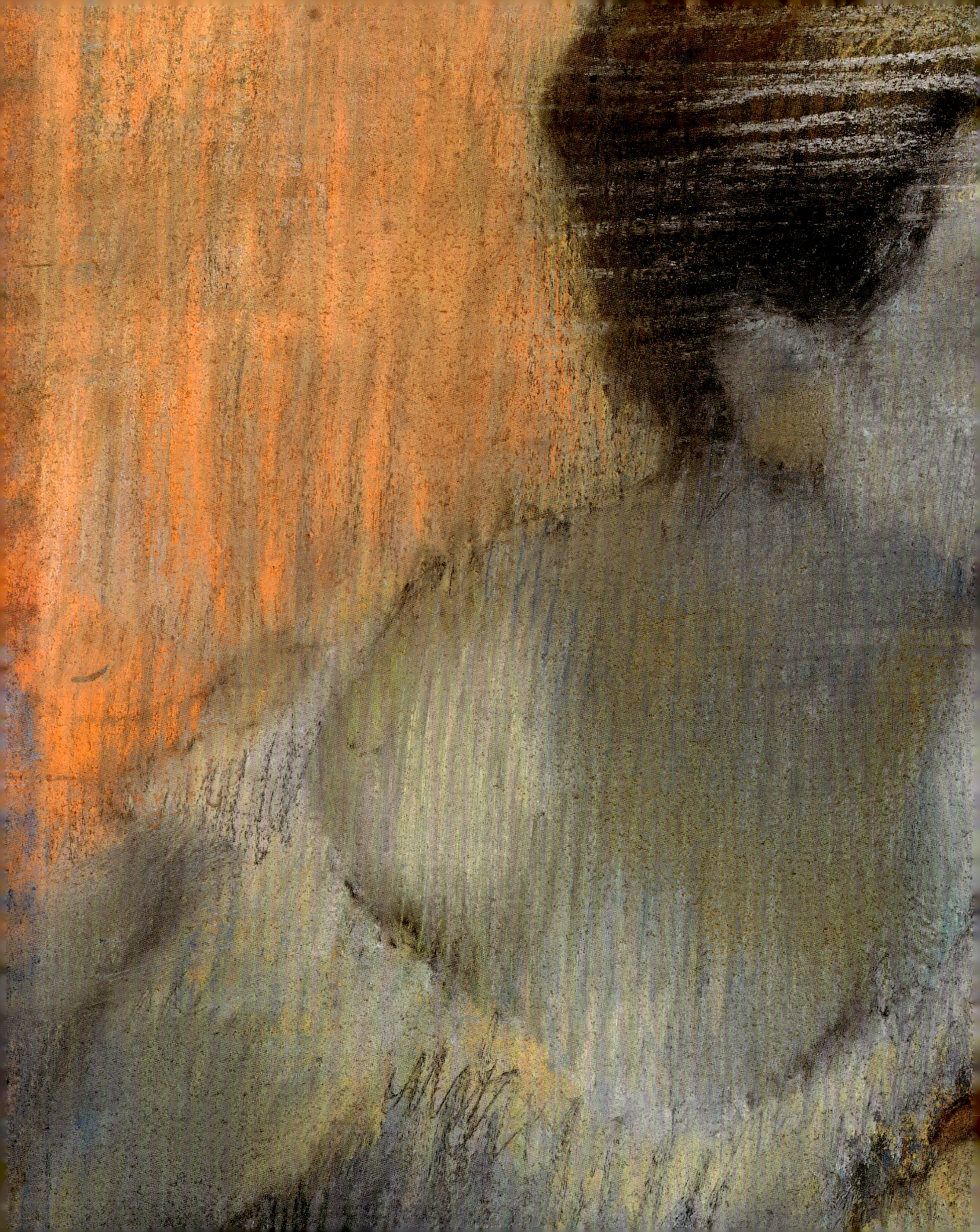

of unintentionally blending it into the underlayers of media. With soft pastel sticks he added thick, broad strokes of bright colours to the jockeys' silks, and with hard sticks in hand he drew long, thin, diagonal strokes of blue pastel to signify rain crossing in front of the horses (see details). The more precise lines remained matt, crisp and distinct specifically because they were drawn on top of pastel that the artist had fixed.

Of aesthetic significance in a number of Degas's pastels is the degree to which the pastel colours have faded or shifted in tone, much like the papers onto which they were drawn. Here again, fugitive aniline dyes used in their manufacture were the culprit. It is difficult to imagine that a pastel that displays the vibrancy of a work like *Woman in a Theatre Box* (about 1885–90; cat. 23) originally boasted an even greater tonal range and broader array of vivid colours. However, examination of the edges of the drawing that have been protected from light reveals that the bright orange tone in the background was once an even more saturated orange, and that these same orange passages were once complemented with strokes of purple pastel that have faded to an almost translucent white (see detail). Although the purple strokes appear to stop abruptly near the edge of the sheet, they originally continued across the background behind the dancer on the left. What are read as strokes of pale brown today were originally purple. Similarly, pink tones used for the dancer on stage in the upper right have faded to white, and it is not difficult to imagine that the headpieces in the foreground figure's hair were also once of more prominent pink tones. It is not known precisely to what extent Degas knew that some of his pastel colours would change; however, given the speed with which many of these dyes fade with exposure to light, it is likely that the artist witnessed some of the tonal shifts within his lifetime.[7]

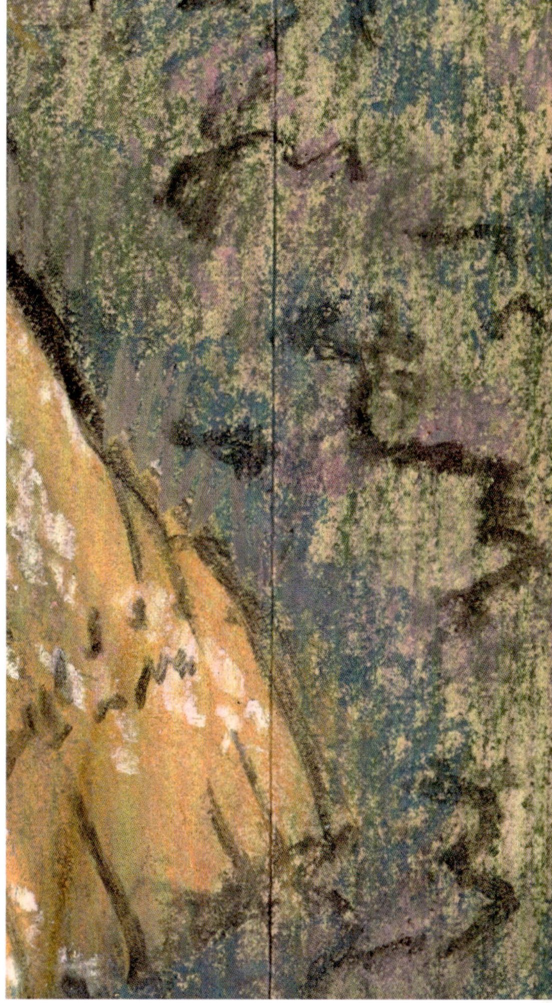

Detail of cat. 16

Undeterred by these inherent changes in his drawing materials, during the last decade of the nineteenth century Degas's persistent and ever-evolving experimentation with pastel garnered unprecedented results. Always at the centre of his production was drawing in charcoal, and when he began to draw with it in earnest on tracing paper in the 1890s he created series of multiple drawings by fully exploiting tracing paper's fundamental attribute – its translucency. Often starting with a nude study on tracing paper, it was easy enough to place another sheet of tracing paper on top of it and trace it. But Degas went one step further: once completed, he could turn the tracing over and use its mirror image as the starting point for another drawing. The artist also produced counterproofs by placing dampened sheets of paper onto the surfaces of charcoal drawings and, exerting pressure, transferring charcoal from one surface to another, thereby creating mirror images of the underlying drawings. He used these methods interchangeably to multiply specific poses, some of which he then embellished with colour. As part of his iterative process, single figures would reappear partnered with others in related variants. And once satisfied that he had adequately studied a pose, or poses, these forms were further elaborated upon in fully rendered pastels.

To the drawings and counterproofs on tracing paper Degas would apply fixative to prevent the charcoal from smudging, roll them up, and bring them to a professional mounter who would adhere them to sturdier paperboard supports.[8] The artist often also requested that the mounter add strips of tracing paper to the secondary supports so that he could return to the studio and extend his compositions on to them.[9] Close study of many of Degas's late pastels will reveal fine, straight lines into which media has fallen; these represent areas where two pieces of tracing

Detail of cat. 23

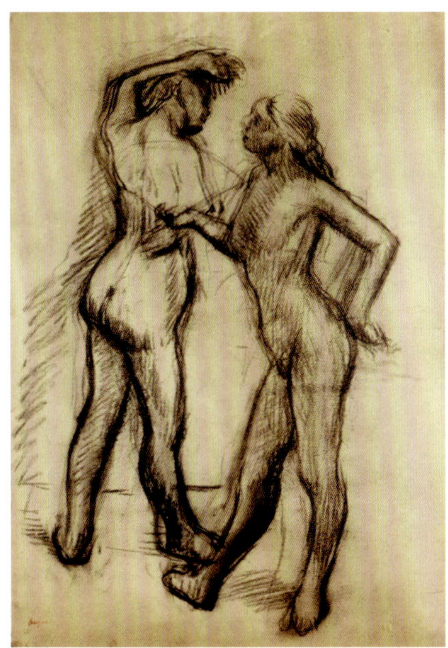

Fig. 15
Edgar Degas (1834–1917)
Nude Study, Two Women standing,
about 1897–1901
Charcoal on tracing paper, 65 × 45 cm
Private collection

paper abut one another. In *Dancer* (about 1888; cat. 16) not only is the underlying charcoal drawing of the nude figure still partially visible, so too is the line where a narrow tracing paper strip was abutted to extend the support on the right (see detail). Once mounted, Degas added pastel extensively to the composition. With the nude well established on the sheet, Degas 'dressed' her, altered the position of her legs and added the stage scenery against which she leans. When compared with a related charcoal drawing on tracing paper, *Nude Study, Two Women standing* (about 1897–1901; fig. 15), as well as several other sketches, the derivation of the traced pose is clear.[10] And in a thoroughly modern and innovative approach to draughtsmanship, Degas made no attempt in these series of drawings to hide the drawn charcoal armature over and around which he applied pastel.

When his thin, diaphanous sheets of tracing paper were attached to secondary supports, most commonly millboard (a thick, textured, grey paperboard), they readily conformed to the underlying surface textures of their mounts. As Degas continued to draw on the mounted sheets, his strokes of pastel would adhere primarily to the high points of the textured supports, with less media falling into the interstices. He then alternated pastel applications with fixative applications, to build up thick, reticulated, impastos of media. *Dancers on a Bench* (about 1898; cat. 13) is

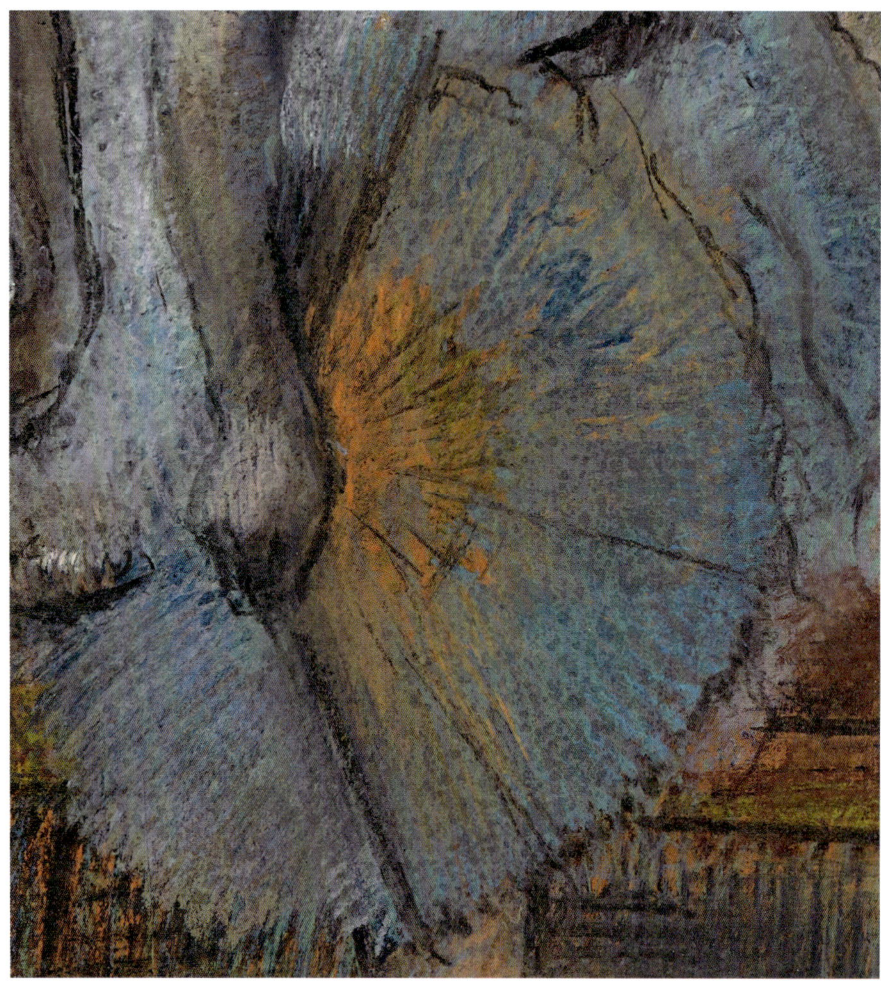

Details of cat. 13

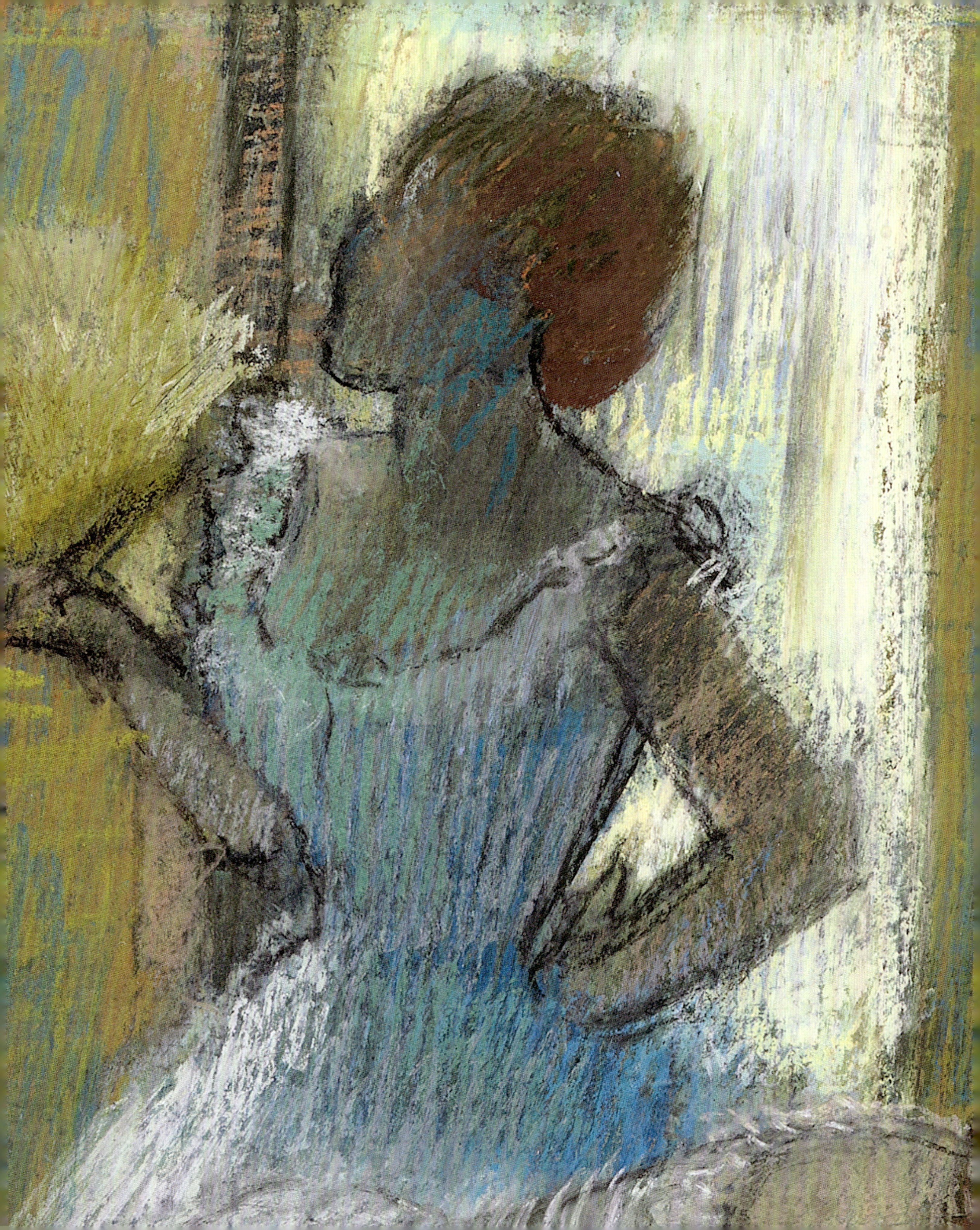

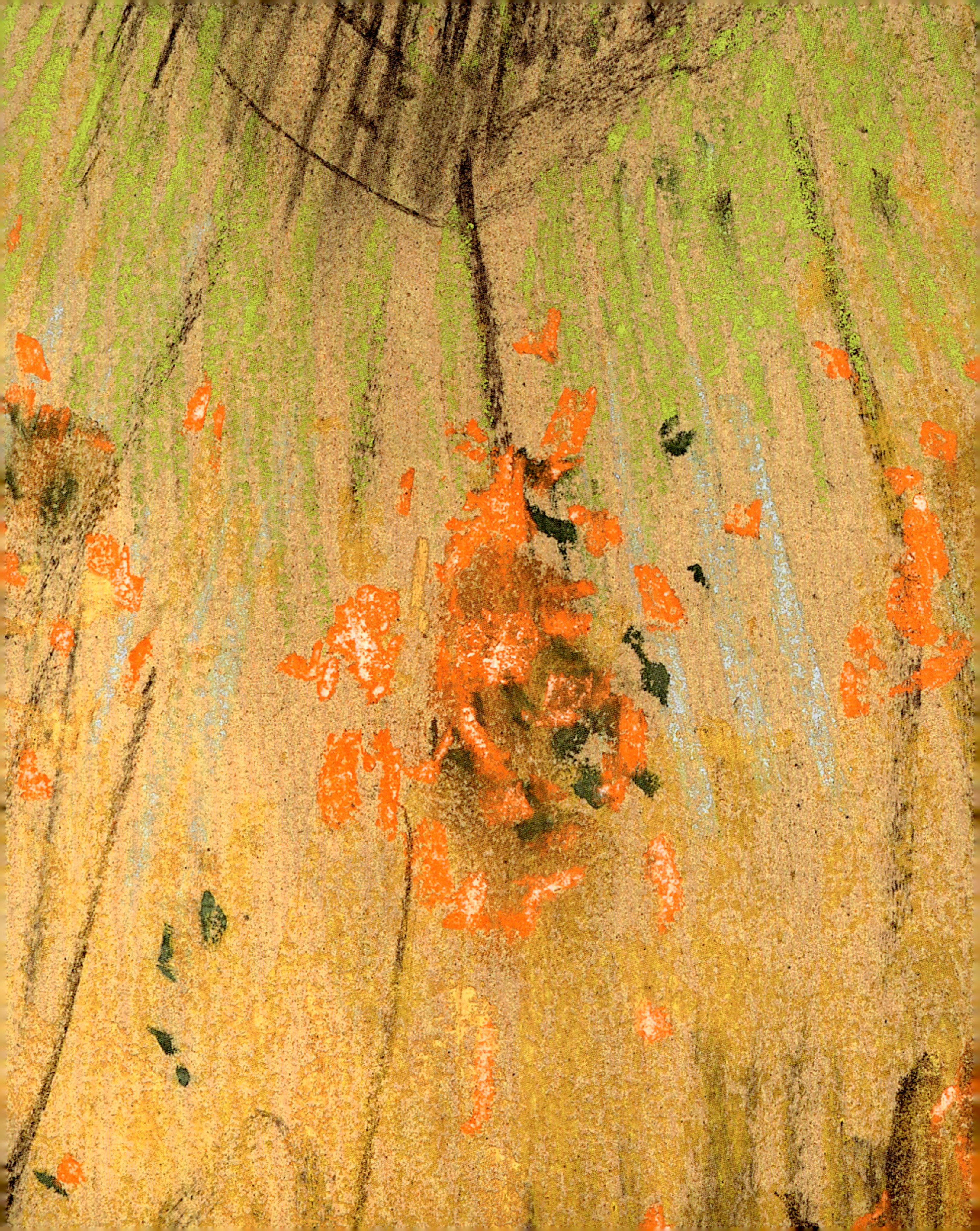

exemplary of this practice: droplets of spray-applied fixative appear throughout, most noticeably in the fan held by one of the dancers in the foreground (see detail), and the pastel colours accumulate in layers of fixed vertical and horizontal hatch marks on a tracing paper support that was adhered to millboard. On all four sides of the primary support, fragmented, irregular pieces of tracing paper were added, and are quite visible, especially in light raking over the drawing's surface (see detail, p. 41). Degas's underlying charcoal sketch extends onto the mount to complete the head and shoulder of the seated figure visible on the right. In his later drawings, such as this, extensive linework in black media and coloured pastel hatchings aesthetically carry equal weight.

The extent to which Degas brought pastel into his drawing practice is well represented by examples in the Burrell Collection. While many are fully realised pastels in which the interplay of broad swathes of colour serve to establish the composition, as in *Woman in a Tub* (1896–1901; cat. 25), in other pastels, such as *Three Dancers* (about 1900–5; cat. 17), rigorous draughtsmanship predominates. In *Woman in a Tub* the artist densely layered pastel in four geometrically distinct and tonally dissonant zones to create an almost abstract composition. He eschewed the use of linework, which he could easily have added to more emphatically situate the figure in a three-dimensional space had he wished to do so. But in *Three Dancers* the pastel is subordinate to the formal structure that the artist confidently established with linework drawn in charcoal and black pastel. In works such as this, pastel colours serve a decorative function rather than a descriptive one. When using his sticks of pastel for the purpose of adding decorative flourishes, Degas modified their working properties by dipping the tips in water to soften them to a paste-like consistency that he could apply more thickly by dabbing short, wetted strokes of pastel on to the paper (see detail, p. 42).

It is not known whether Burrell intentionally sought out pastels and charcoal drawings from pivotal moments in Degas's explorations with these media. Whether deliberately or by chance, the pastels that fell into Burrell's hands provide an extraordinarily rich and comprehensive group that is illustrative of the material turns that helped to shape the artist's drawing practices. From the drawings themselves, a chronology of Degas's use of various materials and techniques emerges from within his collection. Likewise, the artist's choices can be seen within the context of the availability of new materials provided by an ever-growing art supplies market, one that encouraged the kind of experimentation that Degas advanced throughout the course of his career.

Detail of cat. 17

NOTES

1 Scientific analysis of three of Degas's pastels in the collection of the National Gallery of Canada identified additions of kaolin and calcium carbonate to the pigmented sticks. See Anne Maheux, *Degas Pastels*, exh. cat., Ottawa 1988, pp. 90–3.
2 Richard Kendall, *Beyond Impressionism*, London 1996, p. 81.
3 For Degas's use of green see Harriet K. Stratis, 'Innovation and tradition in Mary Cassatt's pastels: A study of her methods and materials', in *Mary Cassatt: Modern Woman*, ed. J. Barter, Chicago 1998, pp. 216–17.
4 Examination of many of Degas's drawings under magnification reveals that he used natural charcoals, which disperse easily and produce soft grey or light black lines. He also used fabricated charcoals, which combine lesser amounts of charcoal with black pigment and graphite during manufacture, to produces dense, dark, black lines. Often Degas used both types of charcoal, as well as fabricated chalk, in a single drawing. For a comprehensive discussion of these materials see Timothy David Mayhew, '*Dessin au fusain*: Nineteenth-century charcoal drawing materials and techniques', in *Noir: The Romance of Black in Nineteenth-Century French Drawings and Prints*, ed. L. Hendrix, Los Angeles 2016, pp. 125–52.
5 This was ascertained by comparing the edges of the secondary support that were once toned to match the colour of the unfaded primary support.
6 Degas appears to have used a limited variety of fixatives that were mostly resin based and possibly casein based. For the most comprehensive discussion of Degas's use of fixatives see Kendall 1996 (see note 2), p. 98.
7 Maheux 1988 (see note 1), pp. 41–2.
8 Kendall 1996 (see note 2), p. 86.
9 In the Burrell Collection there is a small, unfinished charcoal drawing on tracing paper, *After the Bath* (about 1890–5; cat. 28), which the artist had mounted with the probable intention of working on it further. Additional tracing paper strips at the top, bottom and right sides extend the composition. However, the drawing remains unfinished and provides a rare glimpse into the first steps of Degas's working process.
10 Kendall 1991 (see note 2), pp. 72–3.

MODERN LIFE

1 *Woman looking through Field Glasses*

About 1869
Pencil and oil (*essence*) on paper
32 × 18.5 cm
The Burrell Collection, Glasgow
35.239

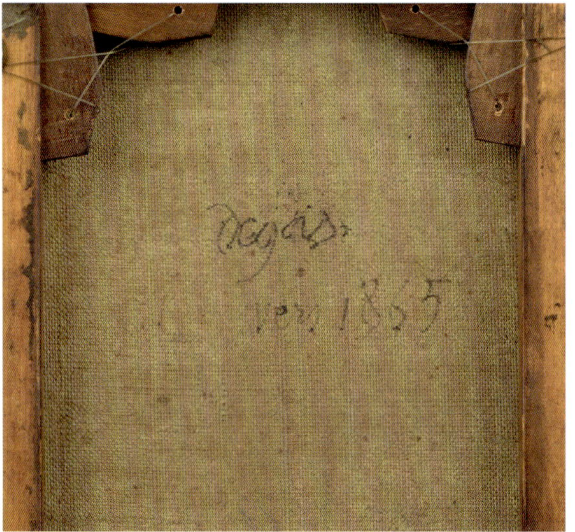

Reverse of cat. 1

This small work has an unsettling quality. A young woman, who from the evidence of her dress and her field glasses is probably attending a race meeting, stands looking out at us. Degas, acutely conscious of the act of looking, was keen to communicate this to the viewer. He reminds us of the need for our participation and also that what we are looking at is a work of art, something that has been deliberately and consciously created.

The idea for this figure first appears in a quick note in pencil on a drawing of a top-hatted Edouard Manet at the races. This would suggest that Degas might have actually seen a woman staring at him through field glasses and quickly recorded the pose. Later, he employed a model for a series of drawings in which he explores the pose, making subtle adjustments to the hands and arms, and experimenting with different dresses and hats.

Looking carefully at this work we can see that Degas first outlined the figure in pencil and then worked up his drawing to a higher degree of finish by brushing it with *essence* (see p. 13) and rubbing the paper with oil. It was probably Degas himself who then stuck the paper on to canvas.

The back of the canvas bears Degas's signature and a date, 'vers 1865' – about 1865. The writing is Degas's own and was no doubt added later, from memory, and it is more likely that the drawing was made in about 1869. The art historian Ronald Pickvance has suggested, most plausibly, that both the signature and the rough date were added in 1880, just after the death of Degas's friend, the writer and novelist Edmond Duranty. VH

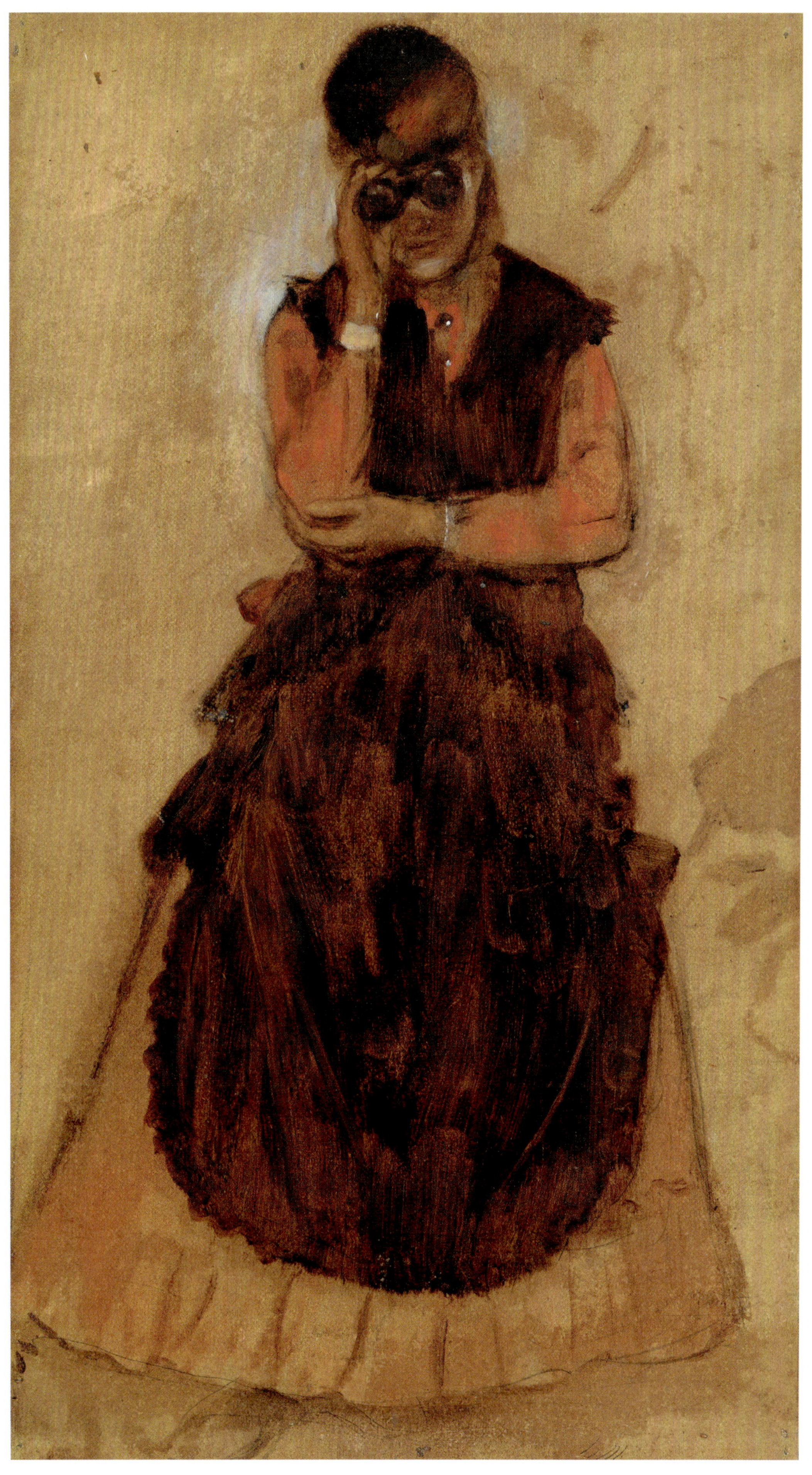

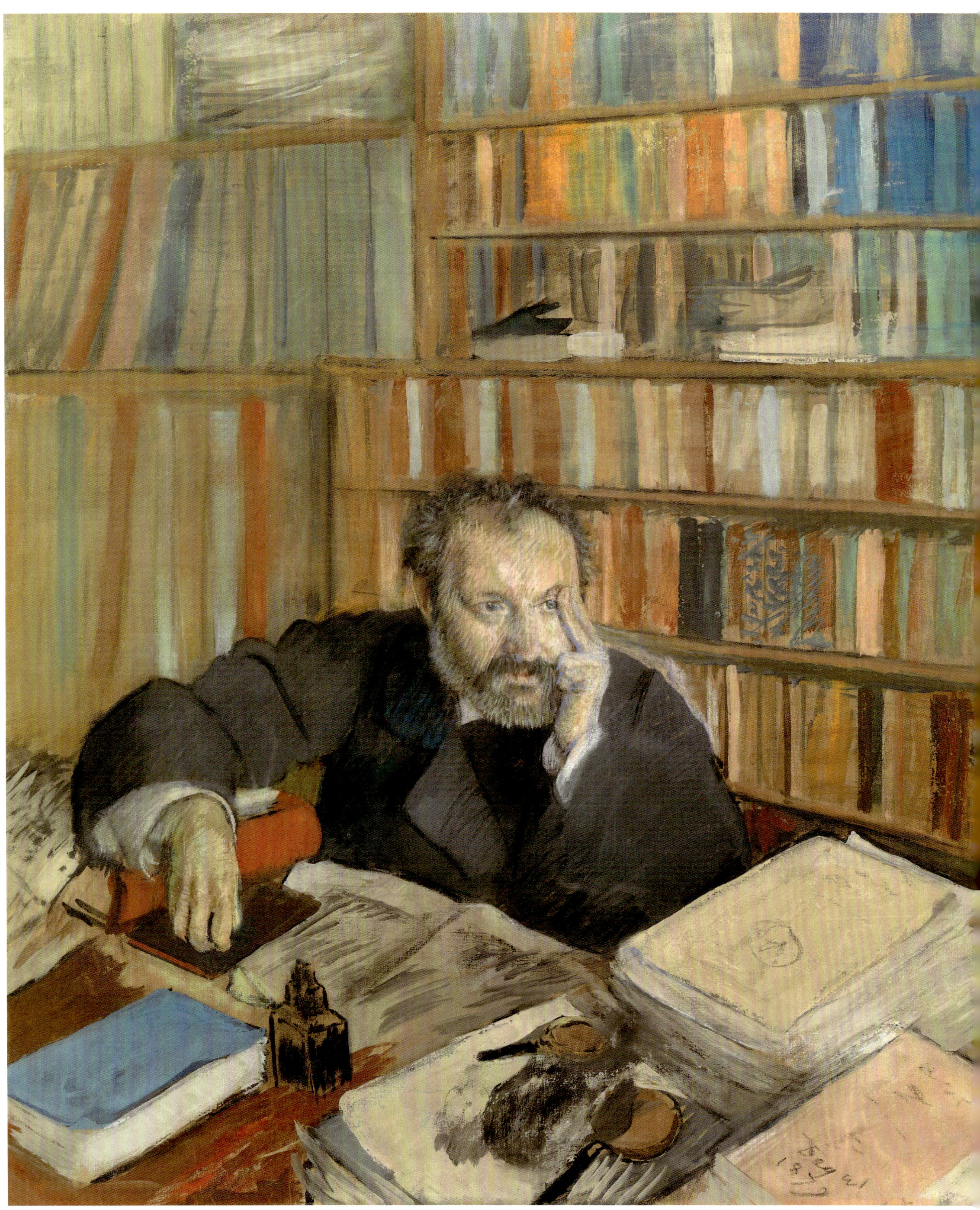

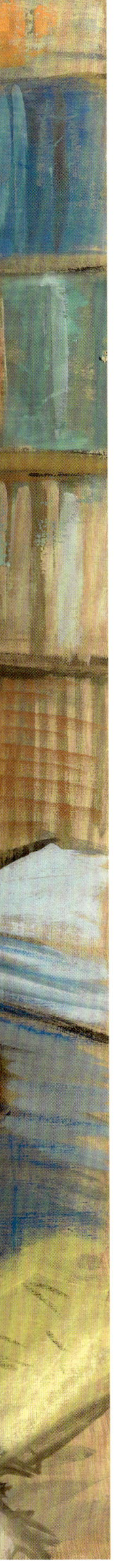

2 *Portrait of Edmond Duranty*

1879
Gouache, pastel and oil on linen
100 × 100.4 cm
The Burrell Collection, Glasgow
35.232
Not exhibited

Degas painted his close friend, the art critic and novelist, Edmond Duranty, seated in his study, surrounded by books and with his distinctive gesture, the fingers of his left hand pressed against his eye and forehead. The Irish writer and critic George Moore (1852–1933) commented on how Degas captured

> the very soul of his model upon his canvas. He will paint portraits only of those whom he knows intimately, for it is part of his method only to paint his sitter in that environment which is habitual to her or him … With stagey curtains, balustrades, and conventional poses, he will have nothing to do. He will watch the sitter until he learns all her or his tricks of expressions and movement, and then will reproduce all of them and with such exactitude and sympathetic insight that the very inner life of the man is laid bare.

With the exception of the bottle of ink and the two magnifying glasses, the picture comprises nothing but Duranty and his books and pamphlets. As William Wells, a former Keeper of the Burrell Collection, wrote, 'all that is not Duranty is books and all that is not books is Duranty!'

Duranty regularly reviewed art exhibitions; indeed, Manet objected so strongly to one of Duranty's reviews that he challenged the writer to a duel. Both men survived! Degas included *Portrait of Edmond Duranty* in the Fifth Impressionist Exhibition in 1880, where it was reviewed by the Naturalist novelist and art critic J.K. Huysmans (1848–1907):

> M. Duranty is shown amidst his prints and books, seated at his writing-table, his slender, nervous fingers, his keen and mocking eye, his searching, piercing look, his expression as of an English comedian, and his dry little laugh into the stem of his pipe, pass before me again as I look on this canvas where the character of this curious analyst is so well rendered.

Huysmans went on to note Degas's brilliant use of complementary colours, the forehead streaked with pink, the beard flecked with green and the yellow fingers outlined in violet. He continued:

> Near to, it consists of a hatching of colours which are hammered out and split up and appear to encroach one on the other; but at a few paces everything is in harmony and melts into the exact flesh-tone – flesh which palpitates and is alive, such as no-one in France until now has known how to paint.

Huysmans also mentioned 'frames the colour of cigar-boards, like that of the portrait of Duranty, exhibited last year'. The Burrell portrait is still framed in this manner. VH

3 *Jockeys in the Rain*

About 1883–6
Pastel on tracing paper
46.9 × 63.5 cm
The Burrell Collection, Glasgow
35.241

Degas had painted and drawn horses and riders throughout his career. As a young art student in Paris he copied casts of the Parthenon frieze, and while in Florence he drew from the *Journey of the Magi* by Benozzo Gozzoli (1420–1497).

Here, against a rain-splattered meadow, a frieze of five racehorses and their jockeys confront us on a dramatic diagonal, while a similar wedge-shaped area in the left foreground is left startlingly unoccupied. The driving rain – slashing, slim strokes of coloured pastel that unify the work's surface – is unique in Degas's oeuvre.

In this highly finished pastel, richly built up with layers of interpenetrating colour, Degas's use of an asymmetrical composition adds to the sense of immediacy. But, just like his ballet scenes, this appearance is highly contrived and born of much work in the studio, from dozens of preliminary sketches and studies. Despite the look of spontaneity, not a single one of his works was painted directly from nature. His use of a dynamic diagonal, of empty space and cut-offs, as well as the dramatic slanting rain and the high horizon line, are all reminiscent of the Japanese prints that undoubtedly inspired him. Like the Ukiyo-e artists whose work he collected, Degas's own vision involved a new way of looking at the world.

In his lifetime, of course, horses were to be seen everywhere, on the boulevards, in the parks, as well as at the racecourse. Unlike his early oils, which show spectators, carriages and stands, here Degas has dramatically simplified his subject. It is the movement of the horses that fascinates him, suggesting sudden action in one, near stillness in another. The jockeys, whose faces are turned from us, may be professional or amateur, but it is more likely that they are hired models or friends or family whom Degas posed in his studio.

Degas uses a final layer of white pastel to modify the acid yellows, bright oranges, emerald greens and vibrant reds of the jockeys' racing silks. Just as the long, slashing strokes of pastel help unify and flatten the picture surface, so too does Degas's use, throughout the picture, of the pale blue sky tones that appear as highlights on the thoroughbreds' coats and, in the grass, as streaks of rain. VH

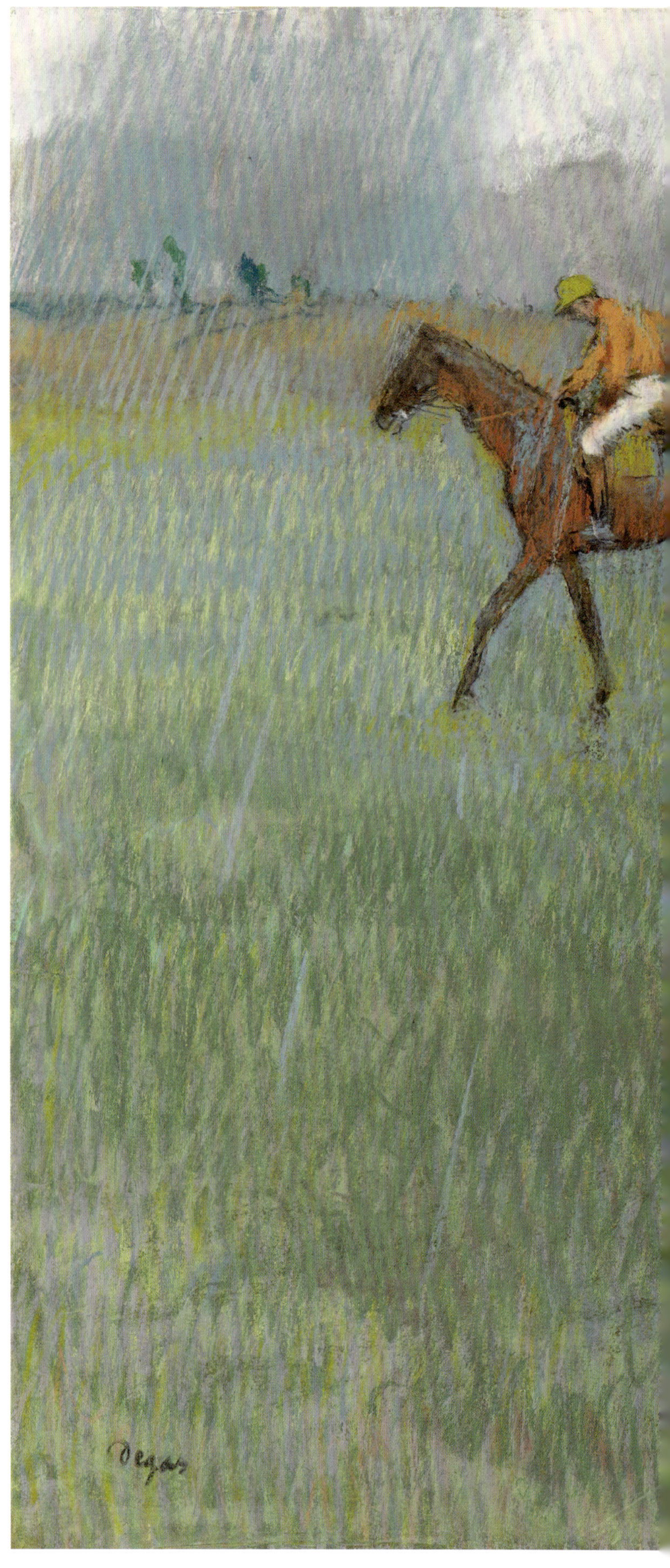

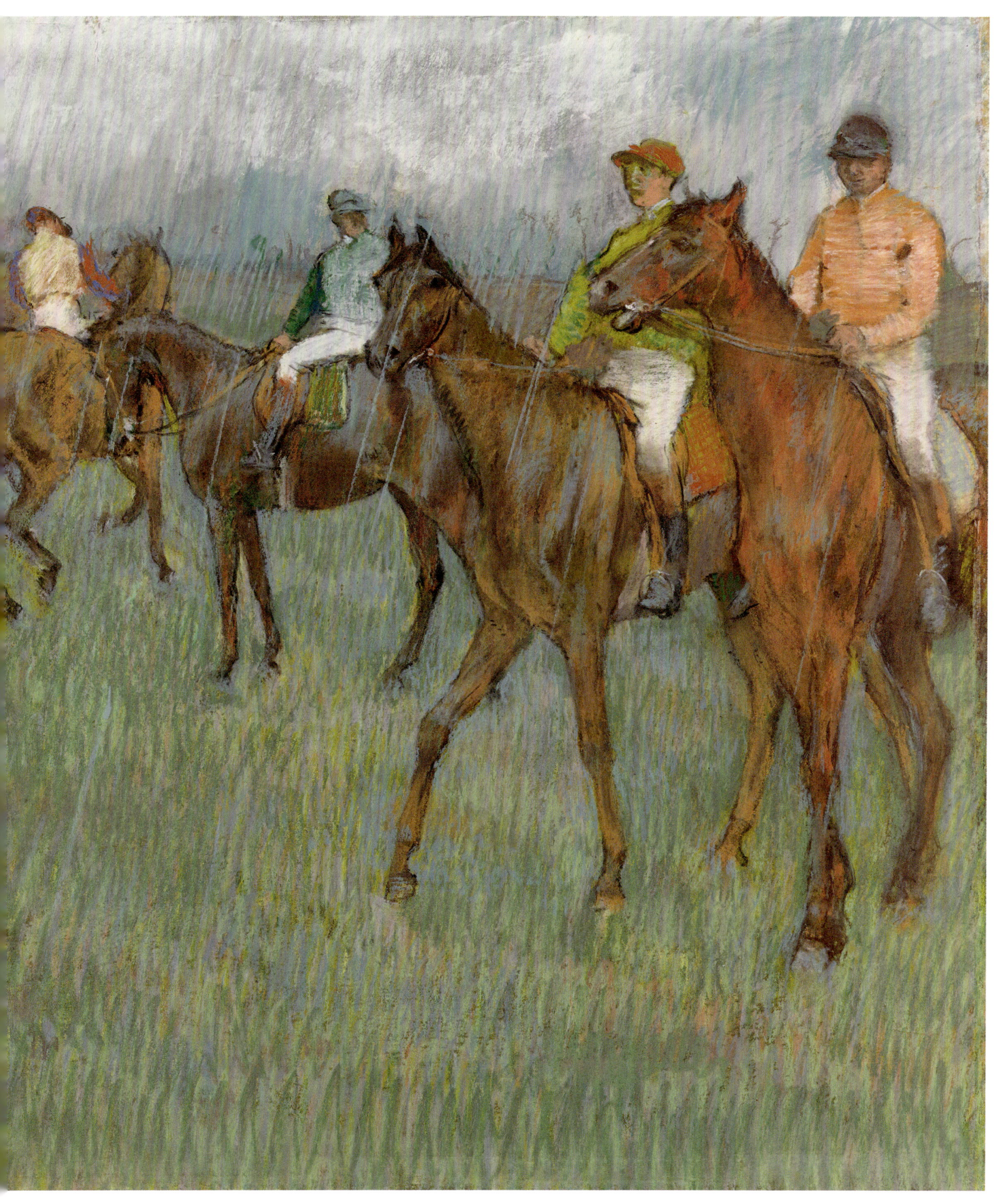

4 *The End of the Race*

About 1882–90
Chalk on tracing paper
14.6 × 19.6 cm
The Burrell Collection, Glasgow
35.233

This drawing reminds us that although Degas was close to the Impressionists, he worked in a very different way. While artists like Monet and Renoir painted directly from nature onto a canvas, rarely making preparatory drawings or studies, Degas continued to work in the traditional academic manner. Before painting a canvas or working on a pastel he would make numerous drawings and compositional studies. He would draw each figure a number of times, establishing the pose and action he wanted. Only then would he transfer his figure onto the canvas or paper support, often, as here, by squaring.

This black chalk drawing of a horse and jockey is directly related to a group of three pastels of horses and jockeys that Degas drew between 1883 and 1900 (private collections). It is difficult to tell which pastel the drawing relates to most closely and so we cannot be sure of the drawing's date. In the foreground of all three works there is a mounted horse with its neck extended. VH

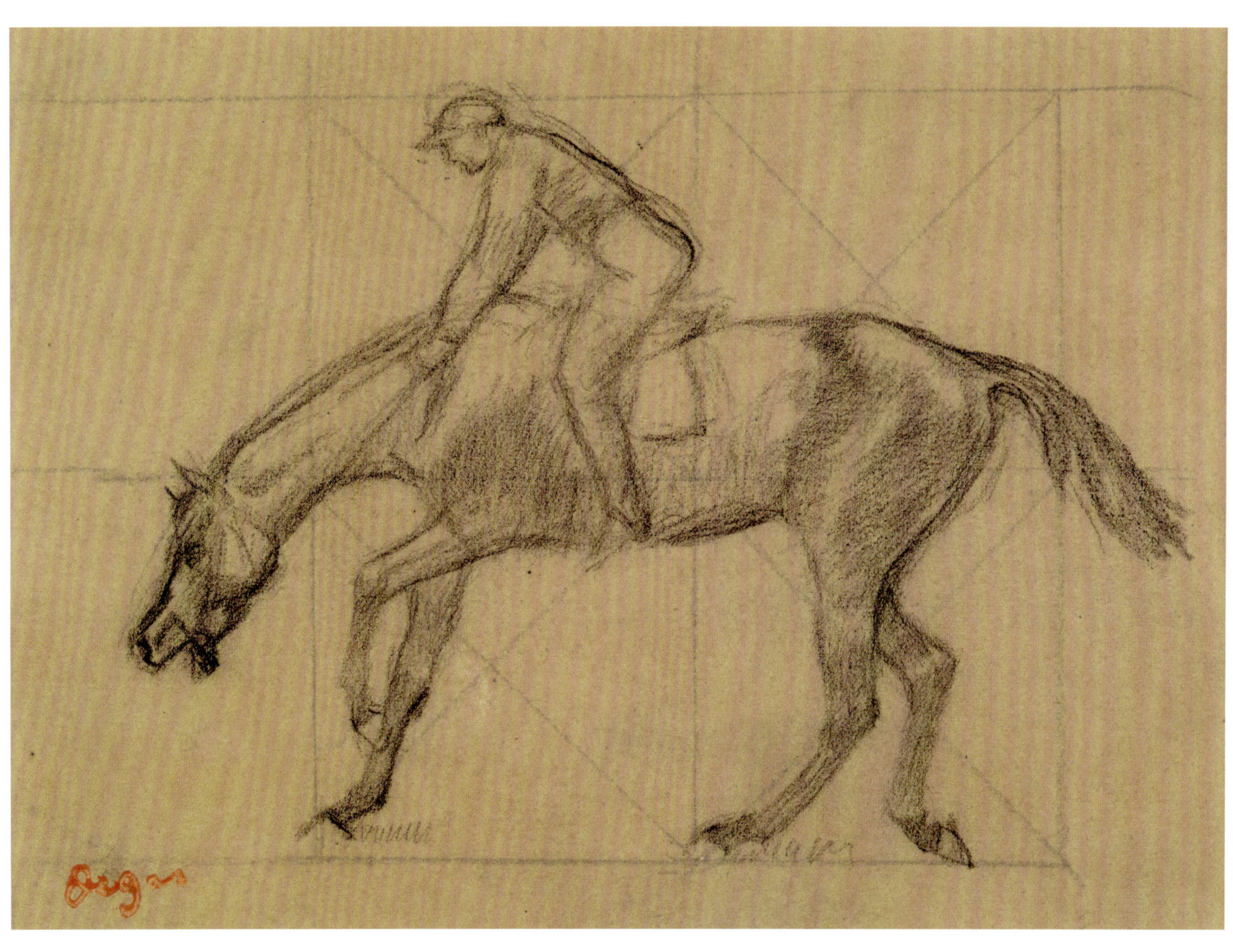

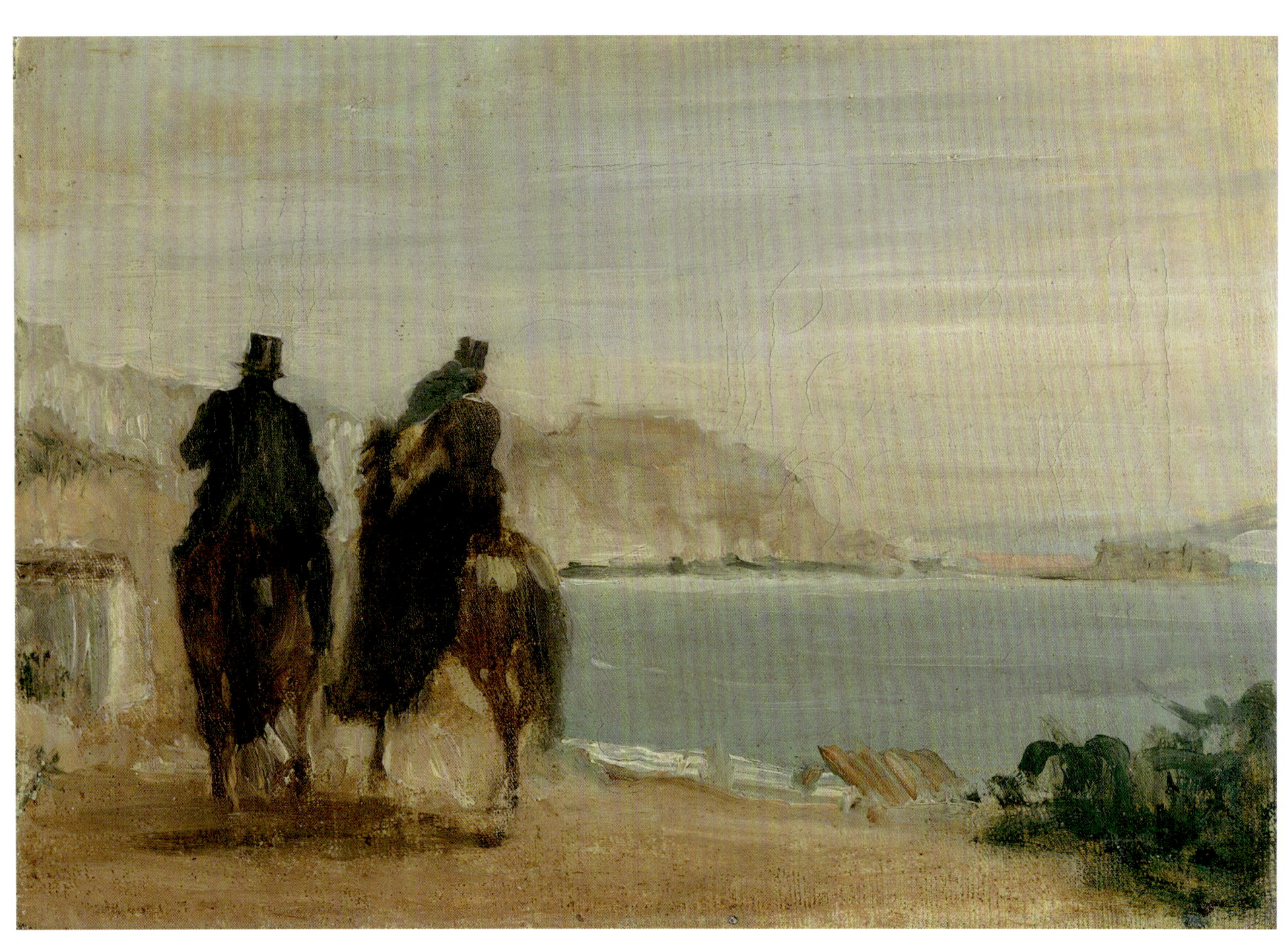

5 *Promenade beside the Sea*

About 1860
Oil on canvas
22.5 × 32.5 cm
The Gere Collection, on long-term loan to
The National Gallery, London
L819

The horse and rider is a major theme of Degas's art. Jockeys, recreational horsemen, participants in the hunt, *amazones*, all make their repeated appearances throughout almost the entire course of the artist's career. He was particularly fascinated with depicting them from the rear. Intrigued by movements specific to given tasks or occupations, he must have realised that the rear view revealed with almost calligraphic concision the rider's control of his or her mount and ease in the saddle. This quick, small oil painting must be one of the very earliest appearances of the motif.

The location is the Bay of Naples, where Degas had family. He first visited in 1856 and was in Naples again in 1860. The painting is not a simple sketch, however, made out of doors in nature on one of those visits, but most likely a studio work, perhaps executed in France upon his return from Italy and combining disparate elements independently observed. It suggests how early Degas began to experiment with what would become a constant compositional strategy, juxtaposing motifs from various sources in new compositions.

Degas sketched the Bay of Naples in pencil, more or less from this vantage point, on the 1860 trip, including such prominent landmarks as the Castel Sant'Elmo, the Castel dell'Ovo jutting out into the sea and, inescapably, Mount Vesuvius. At about the same time, although not necessarily still in Italy, he made a vertical sketch in ink and white gouache of these two top-hatted riders, the woman perched side-saddle, her veil billowing in the breeze. As the Degas scholar Richard Kendall has observed, aside from the broad curve of the bay and its limpid blue water, Naples itself is not immediately recognisable here. Vesuvius has vanished, detail has been suppressed and the relatively large scale of the figures is out of keeping with the vast sweep of the actual bay. We are now at a generic seashore. Only the dust kicked up by the horses suggests the arid south.

The same female figure reappears in a painting probably executed in 1861, where the setting is meant to be Normandy in north-western France (*On the Racecourse*, Öffentliche Kunstsammlung, Basel). CR

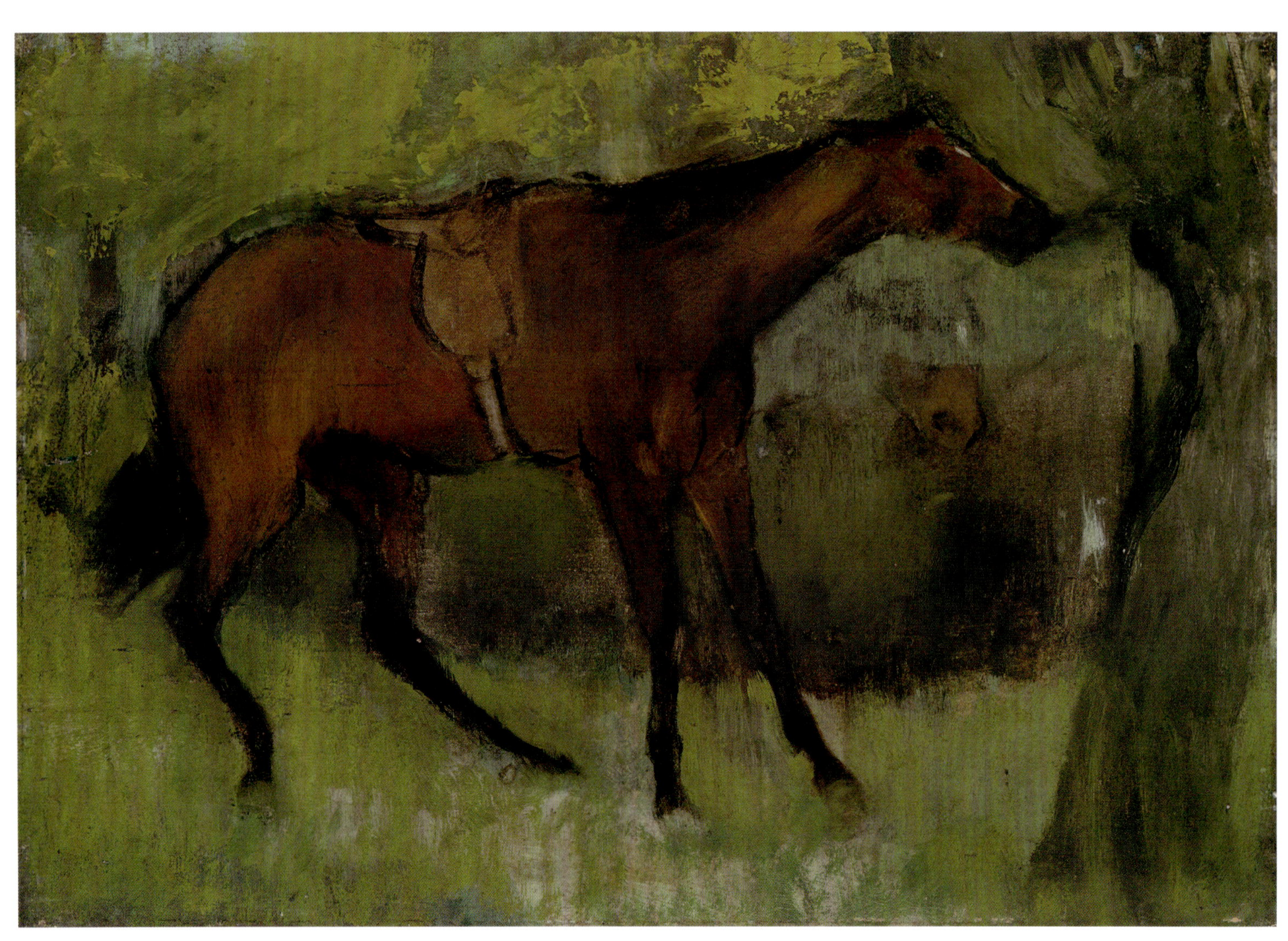

6 *Horse tied to a Tree*

About 1873–80
Oil on wood
22.2 × 31.7 cm
The Burrell Collection, Glasgow
35.240

This small and unusual oil is claustrophobic in its intensity. In a dark woodland setting, a chestnut horse is tethered to a tree. The horse is saddled but its rider is nowhere in sight. Degas suggests the horse's determined character: its hind legs are splayed as it pulls to get free, its head held high. Working from sketches and from memory, he captures the essentials of the horse, establishing its full form with a strong outline and capturing the animal's movement with minimal distracting details. The note of white on the horse's head is repeated on the pentimento head lower down.

Left in Degas's studio at his death, this tiny, unresolved study was certainly never meant to be seen. It was not included in any of the atelier sales, and subsequently entered the collection of Degas's brother René.

Horses feature in many areas of William Burrell's collection, from Tang *sancai* (triple-glazed) figures, through Renaissance tapestries to the paintings and watercolours of other French nineteenth-century artists such as Théodore Géricault and Alexis Perignon (fig. 16, which Burrell purchased as by Eugène Delacroix). VH

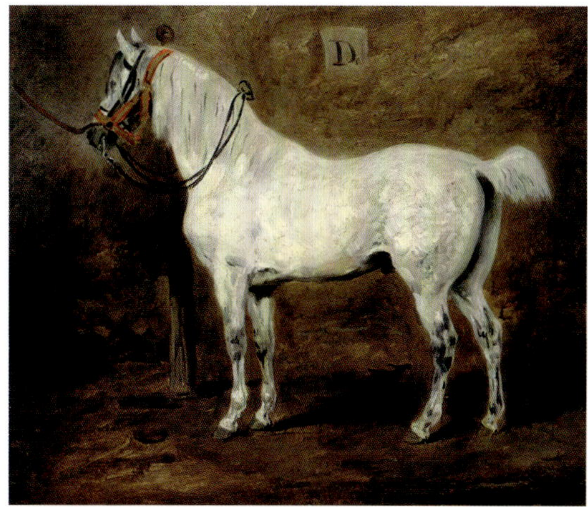

Fig. 16
Alexis Perignon (1806–1882), formerly attributed to Eugène Delacroix (1798–1863)
The White Horse
Oil on canvas, 45.7 × 55.9 cm
The Burrell Collection, Glasgow
35.250

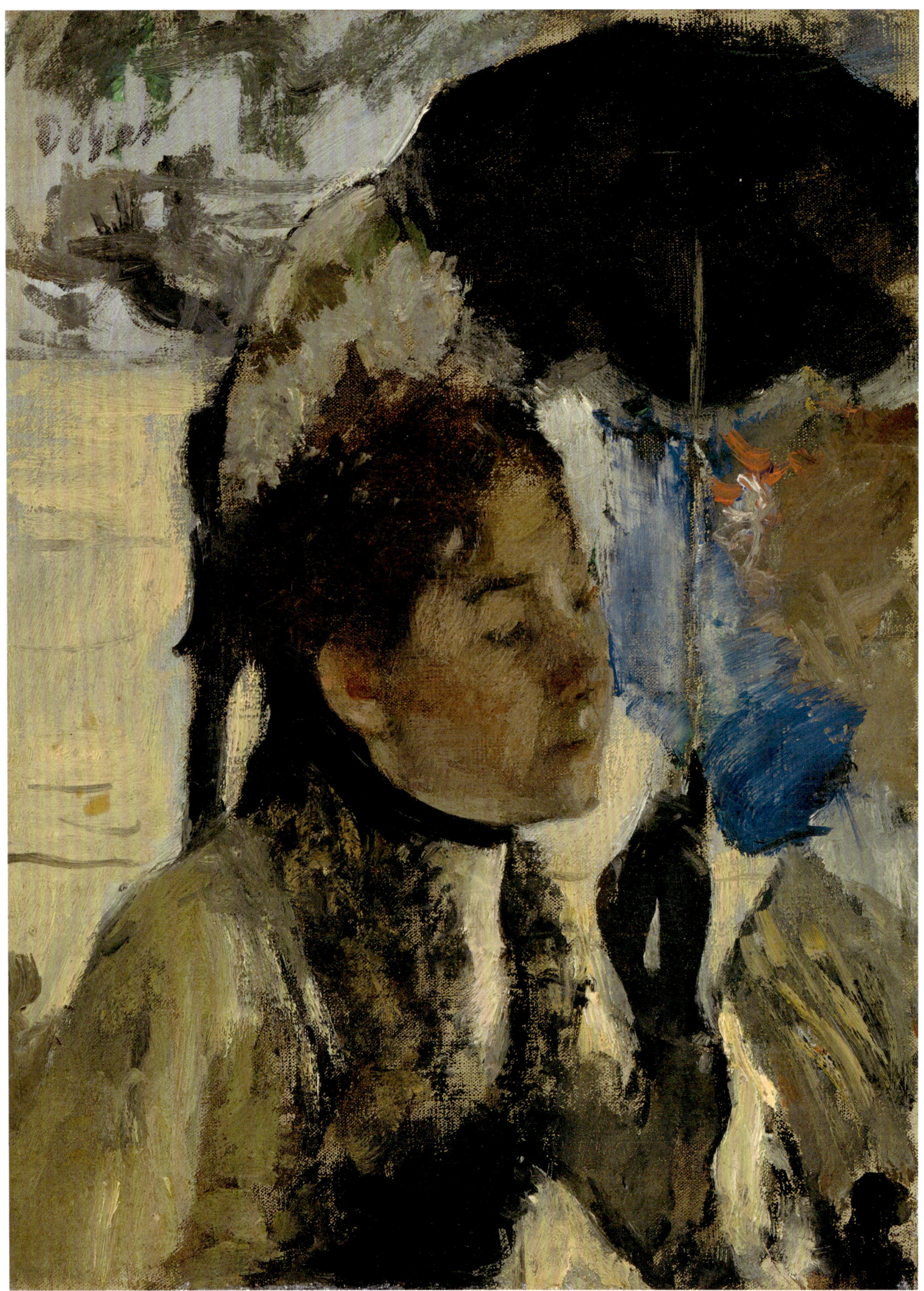

7 *In the Tuileries Gardens*

About 1880
Oil on canvas
27.3 × 20.3 cm
The Burrell Collection, Glasgow
35.234

This small oil is a snapshot of Degas's Paris and may have been inspired by something the artist saw as he passed by on an omnibus. He captures the fleeting nature of such a scene, giving us just enough information to let us understand what we see and leaving our imagination to fill in the details.

Here we glimpse a young woman, her face shielded by the small parasol she holds in her black-gloved hand, her fashionable bonnet perched at the back of her head, with ribbons to tie it in place. Her hair is arranged with ringlets falling down at the back, and her outfit has a V-shaped or rectangular décolletage. She walks with a companion whose parasol and bonnet are evoked by a few quick strokes of red. The sandy tones suggest that these women may be strolling in the Tuileries Gardens in the centre of Paris, or perhaps at a racecourse.

Although this oil was painted in the studio, Degas manages to create a feeling of instantaneity. The painting has a daring, sketch-like quality: the figures are cropped, much of the canvas is left bare and we have the impression of haste. It is only with difficulty that we make out the blur of black and grey in the top left corner, and guess that it is meant to suggest a horse and carriage. Degas's own signature here proves that he was happy with this work.

It is interesting to compare Degas's image of fashionable women in public with those of his contemporaries, such as the portrait of Mlle Aube de la Holde by Gustave Courbet or *The Empress Eugénie on The Beach at Trouville* and *The Jetty at Trouville* by Eugène Boudin, all three in the Burrell Collection.

VH

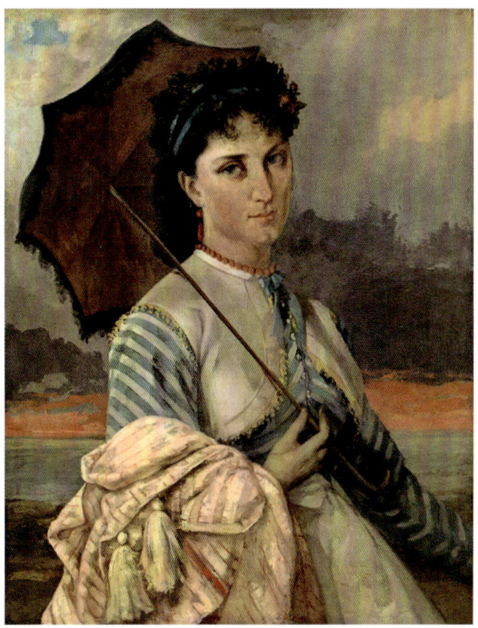

Fig. 17
Gustave Courbet (1819–1877)
Woman with a Parasol, Mademoiselle Aube de la Holde, 1865
Oil on canvas, 92.1 × 73.7 cm
The Burrell Collection, Glasgow
35.65

8 *At the Café de Châteaudun*

About 1869–71
Pencil and oil (*essence*) on paper
23.7 × 19 cm
The National Gallery, London
NG 6536

Two men peruse a newspaper or menu, one with a magnifying glass, the other through his monocle. The first points to the text with his finger while the other clasps his wrist, perhaps to reinforce a point. Yet despite such gestures their interaction is ambiguous and they do not appear to be conversing. Degas made several preparatory sketches for this work in one of his notebooks, now in the Bibliothèque nationale in Paris, which spans the years 1867–74. In these he explored various poses for the men, whether from the front or in profile, but none was carried through to this final painting, which is also on paper. Here Degas has laid diluted oil paint (*essence*) over a pencil drawing, the lines of which are still visible in areas through the thin paint. The thickness of the paint varies greatly throughout the picture, from the sketchy grey of the walls to the significantly heavier blacks and browns of their clothes. The artist has used a pale yellow to convey the gleam of the panelling and mirror frame. Bright touches of white accentuate areas such the newspaper, the collars and cuffs.

The setting and the men's activity are among the earliest explorations of the theme of the café or café-concert, later to become central to Degas's oeuvre. Living for most of his life in Montmartre, from the late 1860s he regularly frequented cafés in the area which were the meeting places of progressive artists, musicians and writers. Particularly popular were La Nouvelle Athènes (place Pigalle, the interior of which is depicted in his *In a Café,* also called *L'Absinthe* 1875–6; Musée d'Orsay, Paris) and the Café Guerbois in the grande rue des Batignolles (now avenue de Clichy). A less well known institution, the Café de Châteaudun was situated at 12 rue de Châteaudun. The street itself, formerly the rue Ollivier and the rue Cardinal-Fesch, was given its present name in October 1870. Degas is said to have given a date for the work of 1869 to the painting's first owner, the writer Charles Vignier; the origin of the title, and whether this was also provided by the artist, is not known. If the setting does depict the interior of the Café de Châteaudun then a date of around 1870 would be plausible. SH

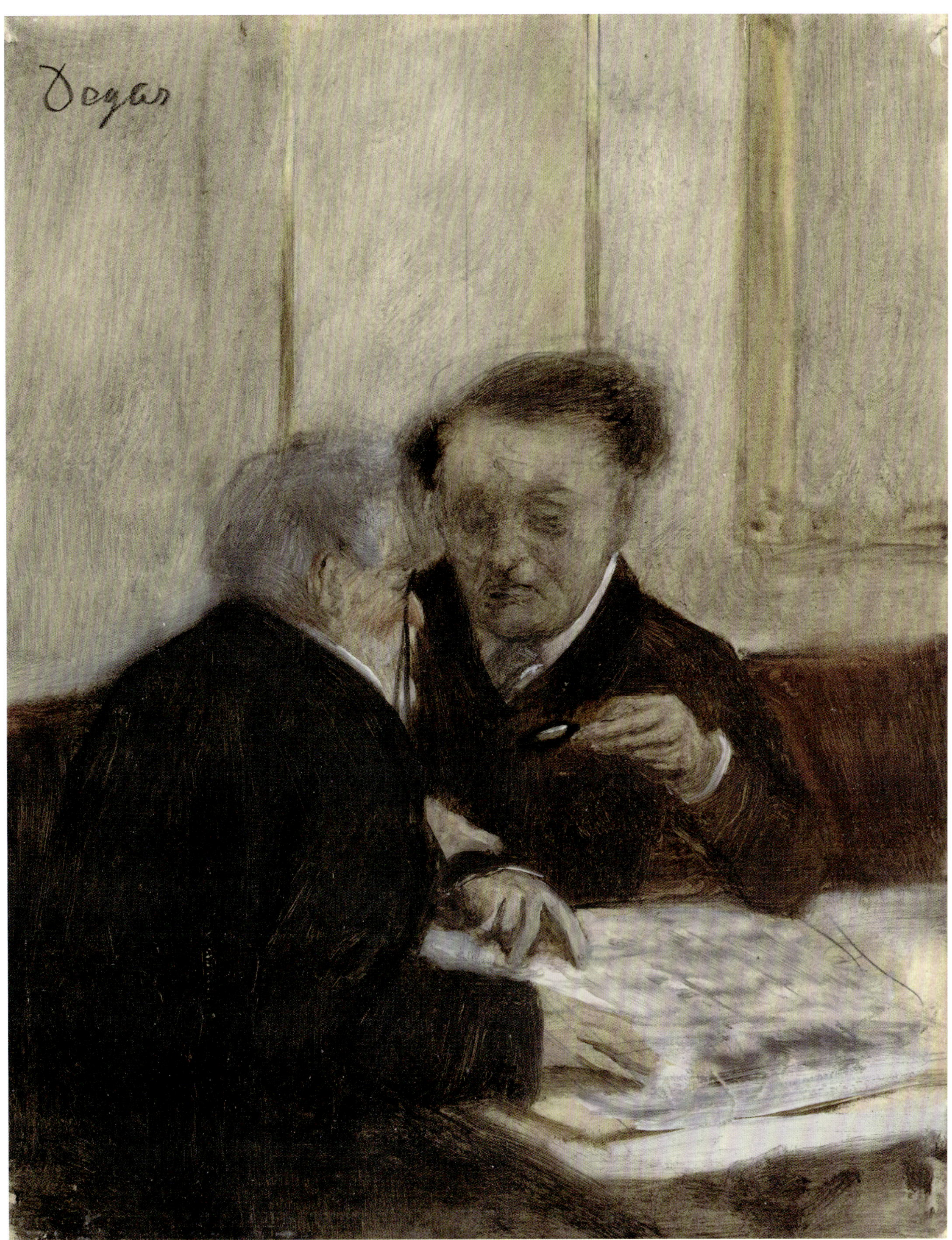
Degas

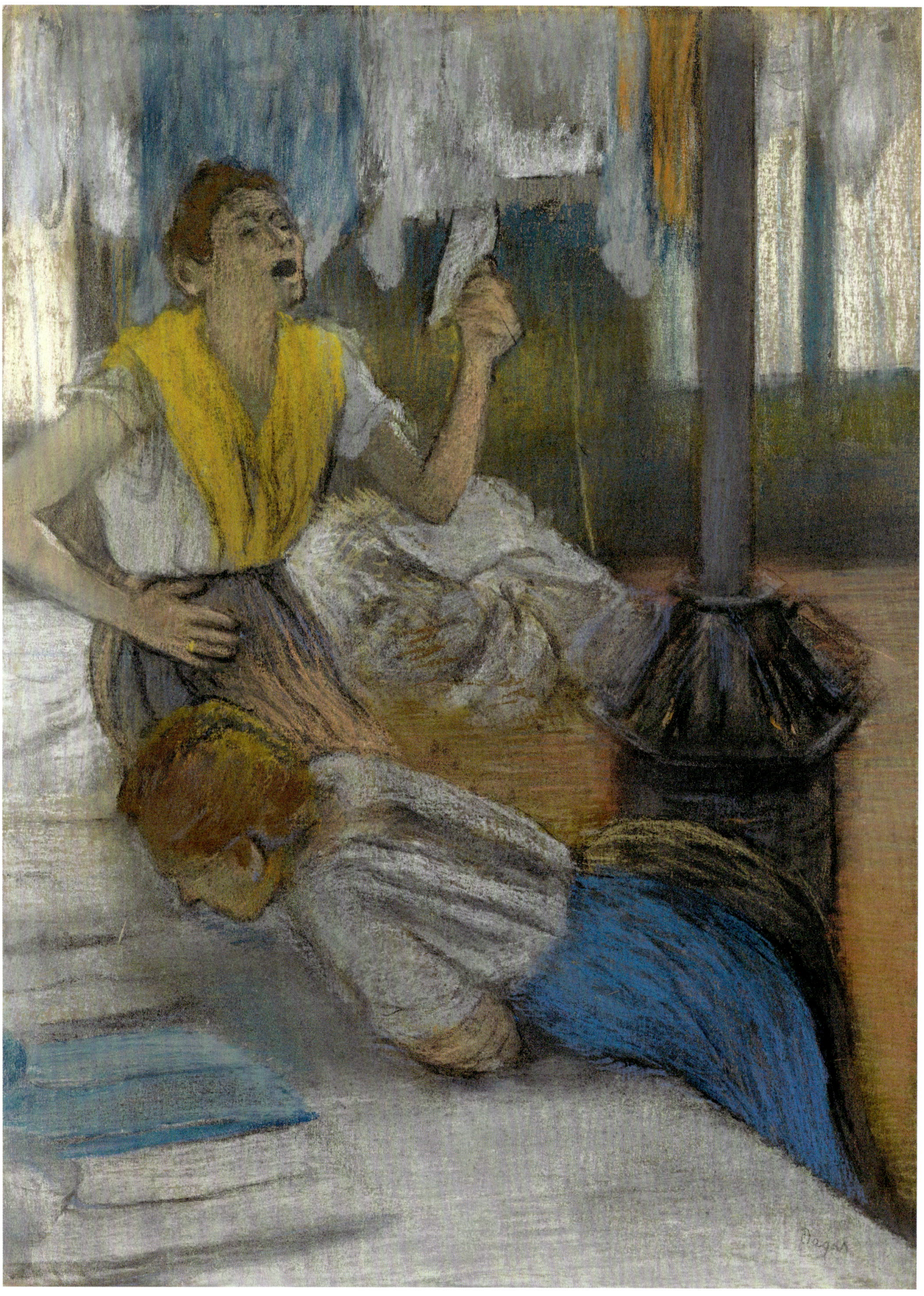
Degas

9 *Laundresses*

About 1882–4
Pastel on paper
63.5 × 45.7 cm
The Burrell Collection, Glasgow
35.244

Against a backdrop of a room lit by tall windows we discern the activities of a laundry. On the floor is a bundle of soiled clothes; washed shirts hang on a line; to the right, irons heat on a stove, while to the left a row of newly pressed shirts have been carefully placed on a counter.

Although Degas was from a privileged background, he often painted the working women of Paris – dancers, milliners, prostitutes and laundresses. He painted these women realistically, scrupulously recording their gestures and surroundings. He first tackled the theme of the laundress in 1869 and would continue to work on it over a twenty-year period. Despite the subject matter, he was able to sell his paintings of laundresses quite easily, possibly because the laundress was a familiar figure in the literature and popular imagery of his day. In Emile Zola's 1877 novel *L'Assommoir* and in the novels of the Goncourt brothers the lives of housemaids and prostitutes and life in the laundry play a central role. Edmond de Goncourt (1822–1896) recorded in his Journal in February 1874:

> Yesterday I spent the day in the studio of a strange painter called Degas … (who) has fallen in love with modern life, and out of all the subjects in modern life he has chosen washerwomen and ballet-dancers … He showed me, in their various poses and their graceful foreshortening, washerwomen and still more washerwomen … speaking their language and explaining the technicalities of the different movements in pressing and ironing.

Degas rarely gave his pictures titles: those we use today were given to them by dealers, critics and previous owners. When William Burrell purchased this pastel in 1927, it was known as 'La lecture de la lettre' ('Reading the Letter'). But is this an appropriate title? The perched figure, head up and back, mouth wide open, is certainly reading aloud; but is it a letter she is reading, is she shouting out a laundry list, or is she singing? Unusually for Degas, he includes a specific detail, the gold ring on the third finger of her right hand, which has led some to speculate, unsuccessfully, about a literary source for this figure.

This is one of only two versions by Degas of the subject in pastel, and it is smaller in scale. More importantly, it is his only work showing the laundresses at rest rather than in the process of ironing. For Degas the laundress was a symbol of the modern urban woman, the true Parisienne. During a visit to his family in New Orleans in 1872, one of his letters home reveals his feelings: 'Everything is beautiful in this world of the people. But one Paris laundry girl, with bare arms, is worth it all for such a pronounced Parisian as I am.' VH

10 *At the Jeweller's*

About 1887
Pastel on paper
71.2 × 49 cm
The Burrell Collection, Glasgow
35.228

Degas, who never married, often accompanied his female friends, like the American artist Mary Cassatt (1844–1926) or the famous ballerina Rosita Mauri (1849–1923), on their shopping expeditions. These visits to milliners and couturiers inspired him with subjects for his art. Here two women dressed in outdoor clothes sit in a Parisian jewellery shop. On the counter are three open scallop-shaped jewellery cases, and one of the women carefully examines what appears to be a richly encrusted brooch or clasp. Her gaze is attentive: she is not smiling or speaking. While Degas enjoyed capturing two or three fashionably dressed women having a conversation and sharing a moment of enquiry or contemplation, this work is unique in his oeuvre in that it is the only one showing the buying of jewellery.

At the Jeweller's is typical of the magnificently rich texture of Degas's pastels, with layer upon layer of colour added using a wide range of strokes. The deep blue, jagged cross-hatchings in the right foreground contrast with the smoother strokes he used to suggest the skin of the woman's arm.

Degas was a perfectionist. If a work remained in his studio he would be tempted to return to it again and again, making changes and trying to improve it. The medium of pastel allowed him to do just that: he could resume or abandon a work at will. While he has brought most areas of *At the Jeweller's* to a high degree of finish, we can see on the far right that he was in the process of revising his composition. He has partially erased the left shoulder and upper arm of the central figure, rapidly sketching in with brown pastel a third woman to the lower-right foreground. We can make out the outline of her head, with quick lines suggesting her mouth, nose and right eye. Her right elbow rests on the table, her hands clasped in front of her. For whatever reason, Degas abandoned the work at this point.

In the lower-left corner we can make out the atelier stamp: like many of the works by Degas in the Burrell Collection, *At the Jeweller's* was in the artist's studio at his death. VH

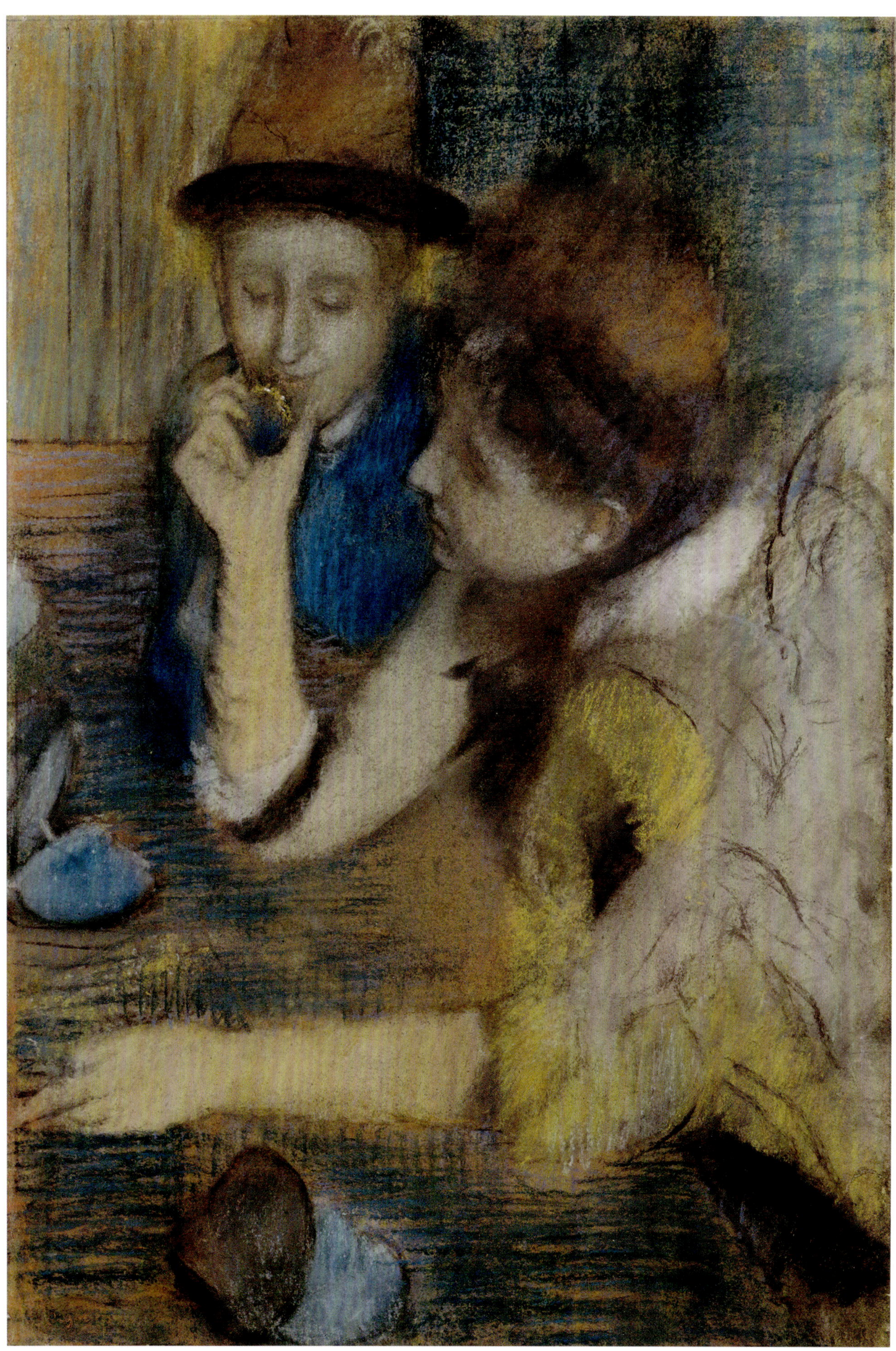

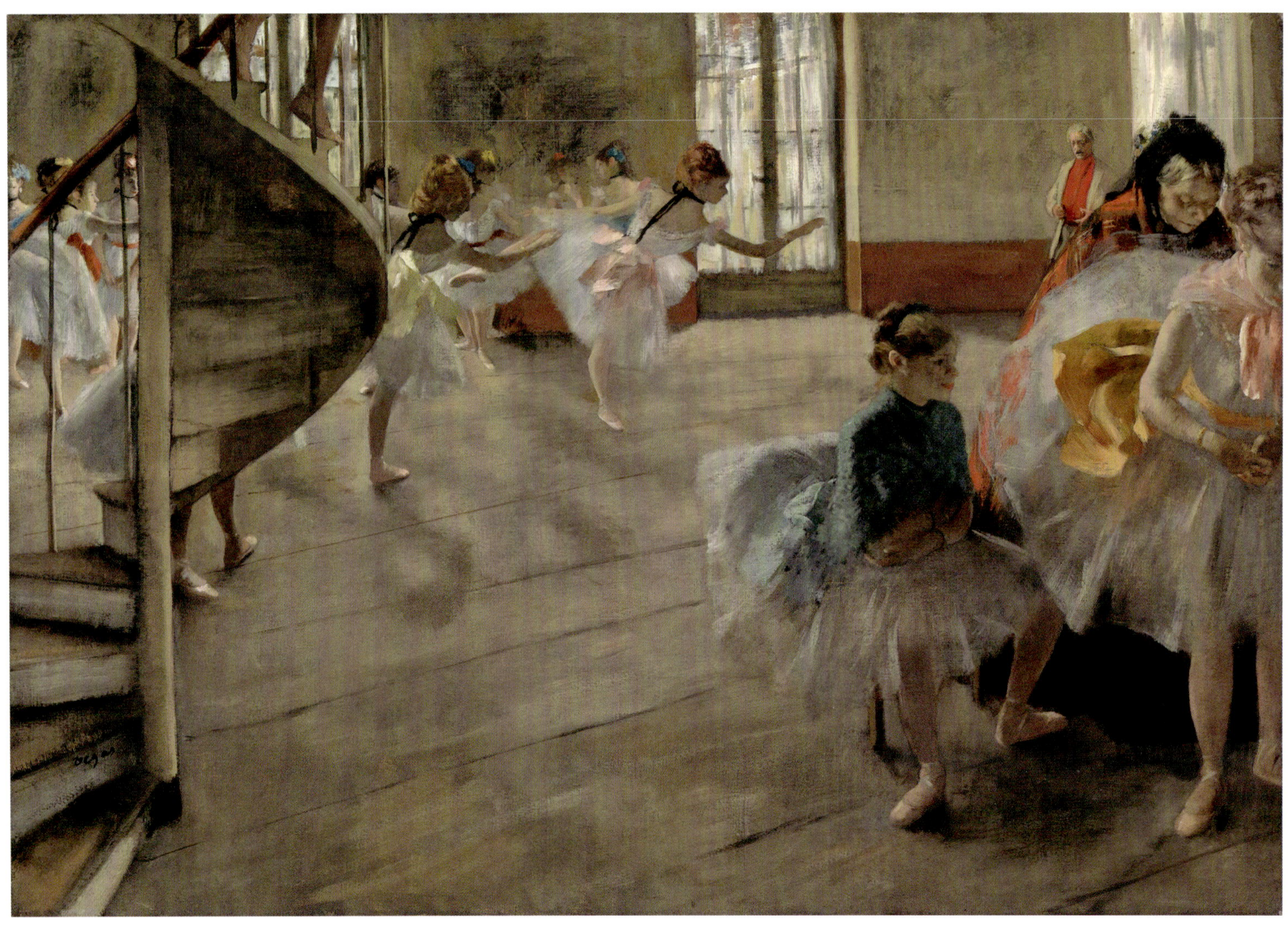

11 *The Rehearsal*

About 1874
Oil on canvas
58.4 × 83.8 cm
The Burrell Collection, Glasgow
35.246

The Rehearsal is one of Degas's first paintings of the ballet, a subject that would fascinate him until the end of his working life.

In a large, wooden-floored room lit by three tall French windows, two central dancers practise the arabesque, while other groups of dancers wait, standing, chatting, sitting or having their costumes adjusted. Degas's use of a deliberately daring, asymmetrical composition with a spiral staircase, down which a dancer descends, is balanced by a group of figures to the right, leaving the large area of floorboards, in the foreground of the composition, completely empty.

Although it seems at first glance that we have just happened upon this scene, it is not at all realistic. As Degas himself said: 'A painting is an artificial work existing outside nature, and it requires as much cunning as the perpetration of a crime.' Here he deliberately fuses the accidental and the contrived, the fleeting and the static, something briefly glimpsed with something seriously studied, to convey the modernity of his subject. The feeling of immediacy, the spontaneous and haphazard character of everyday life, is conveyed by his use of compositional crops.

While it is difficult to know for certain, the setting for *The Rehearsal* is thought to be a room in the old opera house, in the rue le Peletier, Paris. The building was destroyed by fire in October 1873. Degas, who worked from sketches, from memory and from his imagination, never intended to reproduce the room as it actually was. From the evidence of other paintings we know, he added windows, pilasters or columns, or moved or omitted them altogether, as they suited his artistic purpose. He drew the image of the ballet master Jules Perrot from a daguerreotype that had been taken in St Petersburg in 1861. X-radiographs of the canvas suggest that Perrot was introduced as an afterthought, Degas having to paint out a column to accommodate him. The solid figure of a woman clad in bright red tartan is probably Degas's housekeeper, Sabine Neyt, whom he often used as a model.

The Rehearsal may be the painting that Edmond de Goncourt saw in Degas's studio in February 1874, which he described in his Journal:

> It is a world of pink and white, of female flesh in lawn and gauze, the most delightful pretext for using pale, soft tints … It is the foyer de la danse, with the fantastic silhouette of the dancer's legs descending a little staircase seen against a lighted window, with the unexpected touch of red from a tartan in the midst of all these ballooning white clouds, with the rascally repoussoir of a ridiculous ballet-master.
>
> … And there before you, caught off guard, is the graceful twisting of the movements and gestures of the little ape-girls. The painter shows you his pictures, adding to his explanation from time to time by miming a *développement*, by imitating, with the expression of the dancers, one of their arabesques. And it really is very funny to see him, up on point, his arms rounded, mixing the aesthetic of the dance master with the aesthetic of the painter. VH

12 *Preparation for the Class*

About 1877
Pastel on paper
58 × 83 cm
The Burrell Collection, Glasgow
35.238

During the nineteenth century the opera was part of an upper-class Parisian's daily life. Although full-length ballets were performed, it was more usual for shorter ballet sequences to be included as interludes in an opera. Degas, whose family and friends included musicians, dancers and actors, regularly attended the opera.

Half of Degas's output, about two thousand pastels and paintings, are of the ballet. He was the only major artist to tackle the theme, which allowed him to explore the human figure, to experiment with unusual viewpoints, to play with texture and colour and become an entirely modern artist. There were aspects of the ballet that he chose to ignore, for while countless pastels show members of the corps de ballet waiting in the wings, Degas rarely shows the prima ballerina performing on stage.

In this large pastel, eight young ballet dancers prepare for a rehearsal, an audition or a dance exam. Degas delights in playing with the varied postures and gestures of the dancers as they adjust slippers or straps, or practise at the barre, and so he leads our eye around and through the room. There is a wonderful sense of rhythm and movement. Light floods in from a large window, enlivening the costumes of the dancers, and highlighting the pink flesh tones of arms, legs, shoulders and necks. The heavy-set figures of the two mothers, dressed from head to toe in dark outdoor outfits, provide a contrast and a hint of narrative.

Degas's interest in opera and the ballet was shared by one of his closest friends, the playwright, librettist and novelist Ludovic Halévy (1834–1908), whose stories of the Cardinal family may have inspired this scene. He describes a dance exam thus:

> all around, restless, bewildered, breathless, and purple-faced, are mothers, mothers, and yet more mothers … What serious and delicate matters there are to be considered: that the ribbons of their ballet shoes are securely tied, that their tights have no creases and are firmly fixed about the hips, that the seams are straight, the bows properly tied, and the tarlatan skirts puffed out prettily.

The setting may be a room in Garnier's new opera house, completed in 1875 – through the window we can see the distinctive facades, balconies and roofs of Parisian apartment buildings. This foyer, if it is a real rather than an imagined room, must be some five or six storeys up. Although Degas was familiar with the corridors and rehearsal rooms backstage at the opera, his works have little documentary value, as on the whole he invented the settings for his pictures. VH

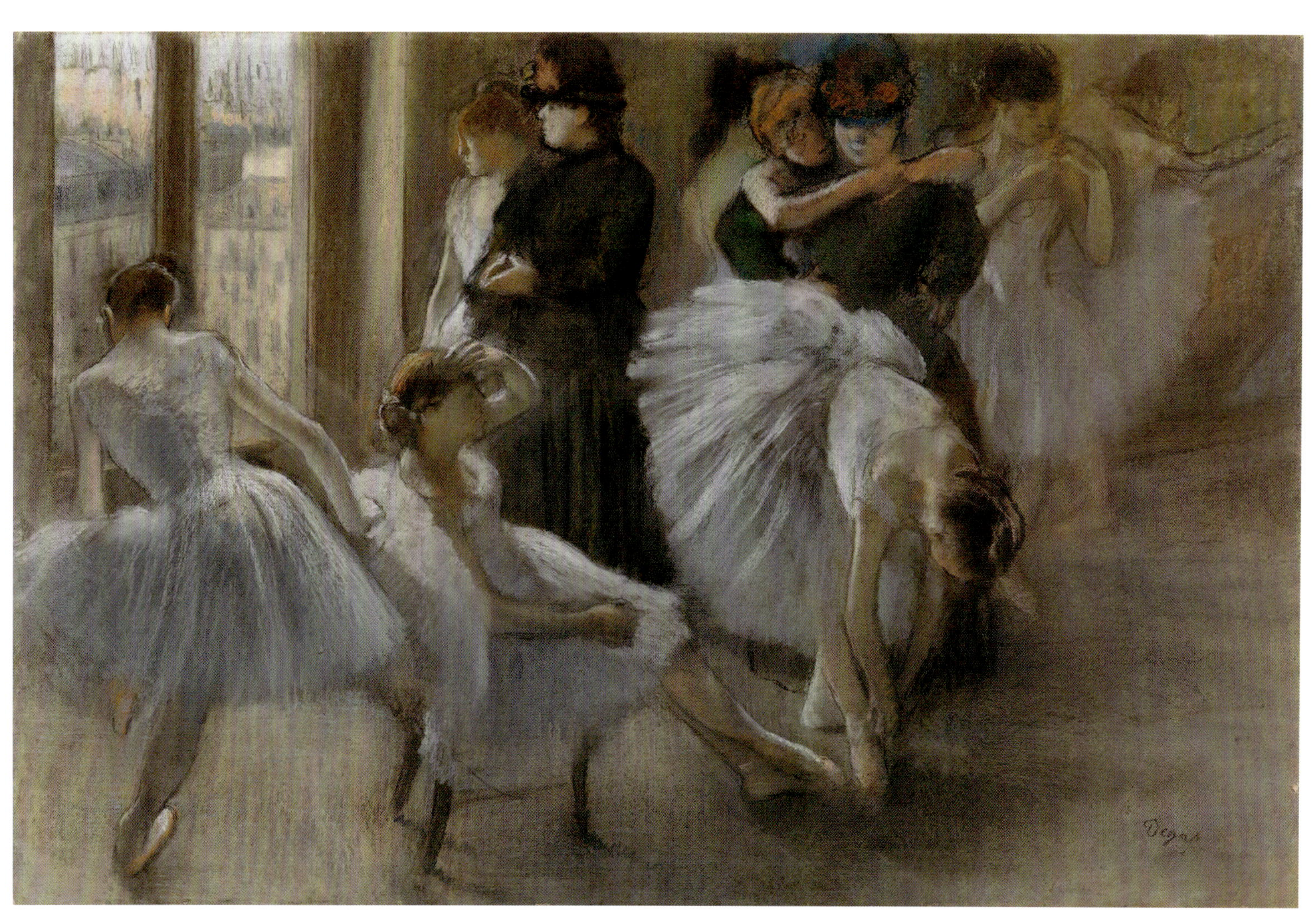
Degas

13 *Dancers on a Bench*

About 1898
Pastel on tracing paper
54.8 × 76 cm
Kelvingrove Art Gallery and Museum, Glasgow,
bequeathed by William McInnes, 1944
2441

Throughout his working life Degas's fascination with the ballet never ceased. This wonderful late pastel may share the same subject as the early *Preparation for the Class* (cat. 12), but the two are very different. Separated by twenty years, there has been a world of experimentation and discovery between them, in both Degas's colour and his technique.

He is still preoccupied with the view of a room with tall windows, with a figure against a window and with the bench that had first appeared in one of his works two decades earlier. The beautiful soft light, the smoky harmony and delicate touches have now become rapid and strident cross-hatchings of yellow and green; rather than gazing pensively out of the window, a dancer in *contre-jour* stands against what looks like a curtain screening a view where the touches of yellow and blue suggest the apartment building beyond.

Like so many of Degas's works, this scene gives the appearance of spontaneity, as if we have just happened upon these four young dancers resting after a practice session in the rehearsal room. We marvel at Degas's ability to suggest immediacy, but it has been achieved by cunning. He deliberately placed all four figures to the right of the picture and quite as deliberately left the left-hand side empty. This is a device he often employed – the same frieze-like composition, the clever use of diagonals and the contrasting full and empty space also appears in *Jockeys in the Rain* (cat. 3).

One startling difference is Degas's treatment of the dancers. They have been drastically simplified and reduced to their essentials with a blunt and brutal simplification of their faces, while the contours of their figures have been accentuated. The pastel is built up, often in thick superimposed layers, long, strident and rapid strokes of pastel signalling the verticality of the wall against the horizontal plane of the floor. Examining the gestural application of the pastel we feel the sheer energy expended by the artist. VH

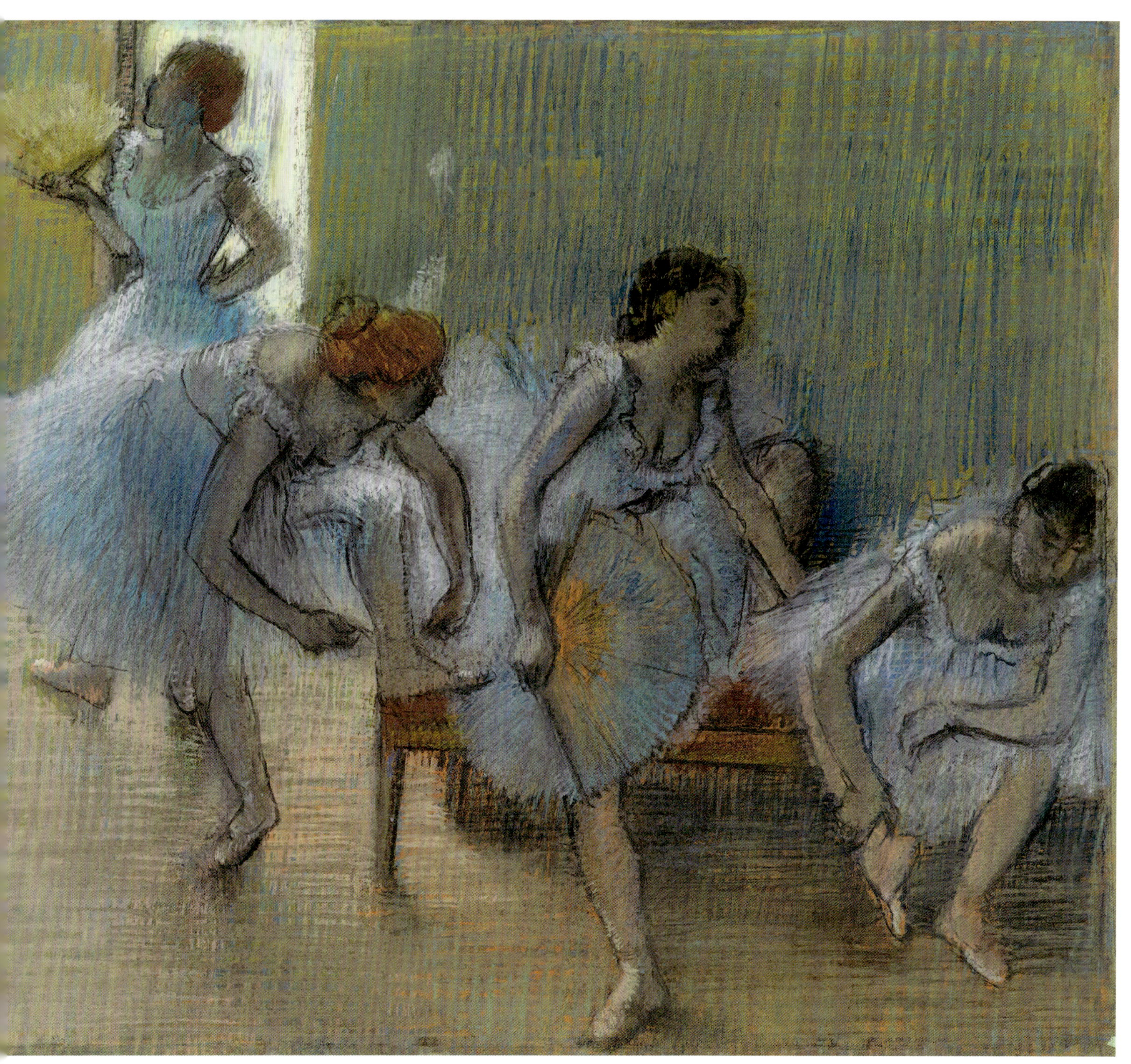

14 *Ballet Dancers*

About 1890–1900
Oil on canvas
72.5 × 73 cm
The National Gallery, London
NG 4168

Set in a rehearsal studio, this painting contains a complex range of poses. Degas often depicted dancers rehearsing, as it allowed him to combine seemingly haphazard formal and informal poses that would never be seen on the stage. A young dancer in the foreground rests her foot on a bench to adjust her shoe. Behind her, ballerinas rehearsing arabesques or *en pointe* emerge out of a cloud of silvery tutus and intermingled pink arms and legs. Beyond them, a large window illuminates the scene.

Degas composed this painting in oil on canvas with extraordinary freedom at a time in his career when he preferred working in the more immediate and flexible medium of pastel. The rough, unprimed canvas Degas chose had a profound impact on the technique he was able to employ and on the final appearance of the painting. Working directly on an absorbent canvas is much harder than painting on a smooth, primed surface. On a primed canvas the mostly impermeable and even surface allows the artist's brush, loaded with paint, to glide across the composition. An unprimed canvas, on the other hand, absorbs the oil binder of the paint almost instantly, leading to dry and broken brush-strokes. Degas used this to his advantage in order to emulate the matt texture of pastel and the quick and short strokes obtained with pastel sticks. The light brown surface of the canvas that shows through most of the composition, particularly in a large area to the right, also resembles the tracing paper that Degas frequently used for his late pastels.

Degas's initial painted outlines for the figures are clearly visible around them. Showing through the matt clouds of pigments defining the flesh and tutus, they give the figures plasticity and set them out against the background. The visible canvas gives a brilliant sense of improvisation and energy to the whole painting. Broken and thick passages of light paint boldly painted across the weave evoke the shimmering and translucent qualities of the dancers' tutus, while smoother regular dabs of green and yellow suggest the velvet of the bench in the foreground. The only fluid passage of painting can be found in the lustre of the bright red hair of the two closest dancers, painted in pure vermilion. JD

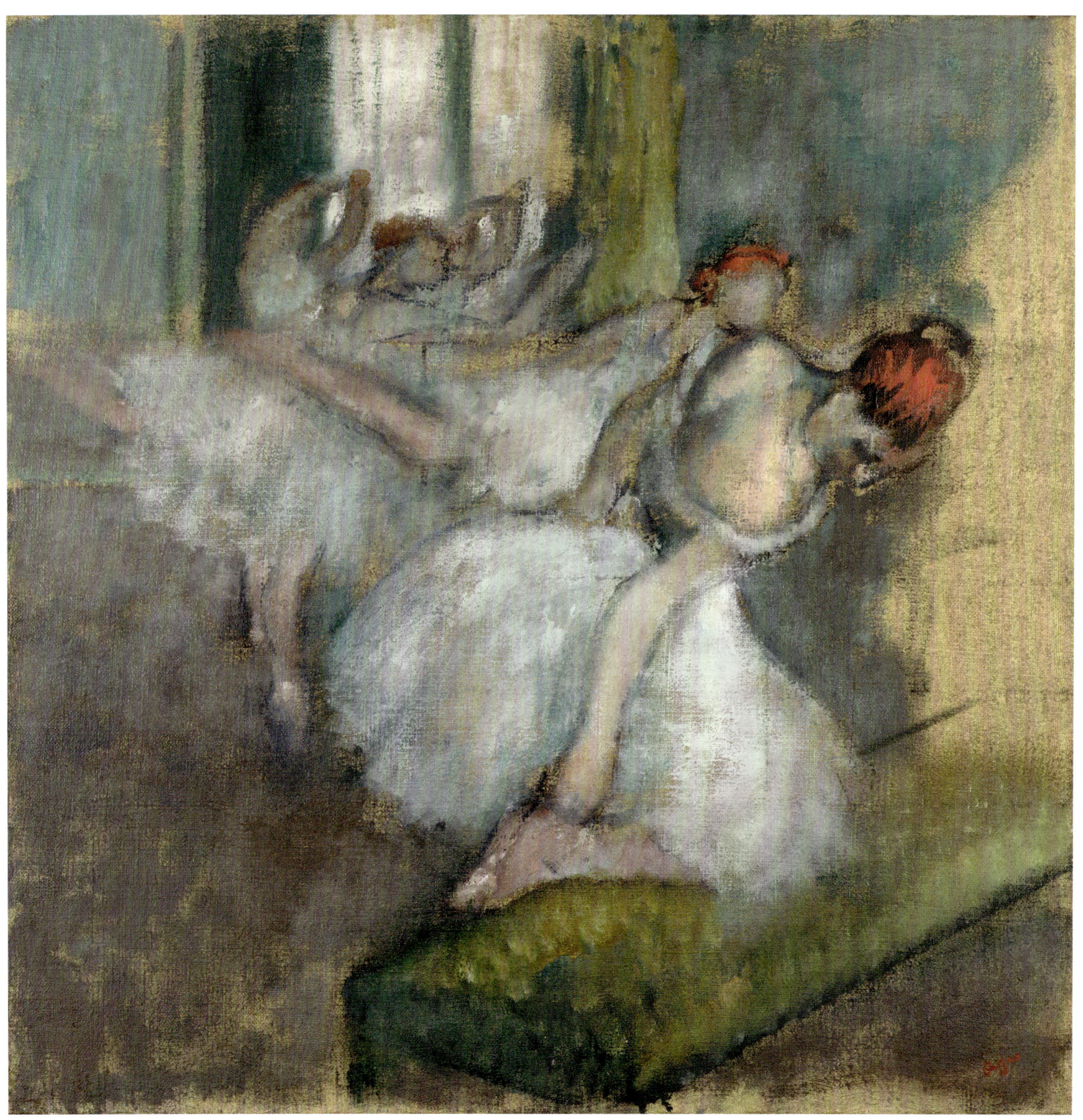

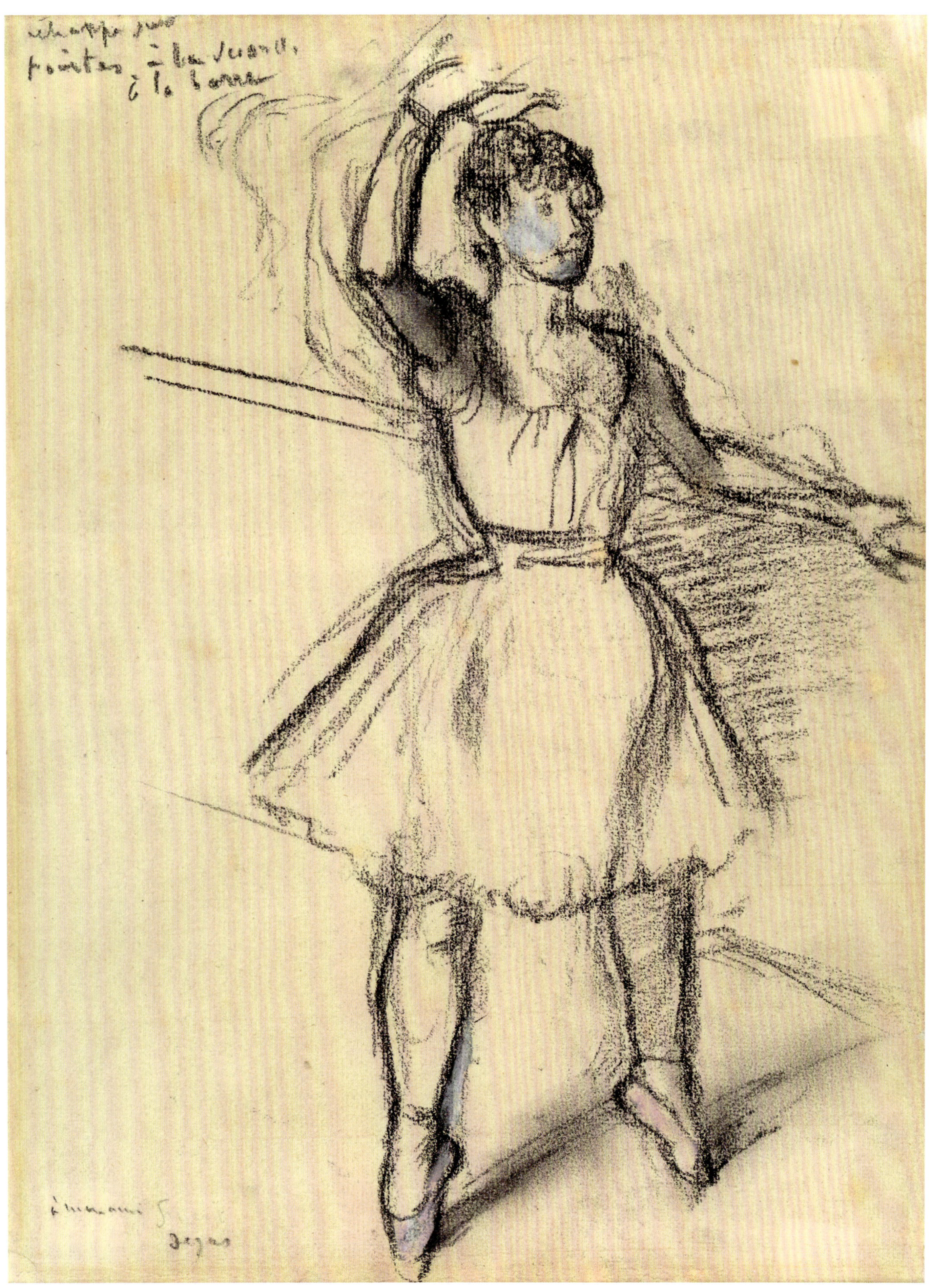
échappé sur
pointes, à la seconde,
à la barre
à mon ami
Degas

15 *Dancer at the Barre*

About 1885
Chalk and pastel on paper
31.7 × 24.7 cm
Inscribed top left: echappe sur pointes à la seconde à la barre
Inscribed bottom left: à mon ami Fourcaud
The Burrell Collection, Glasgow
35.245

Degas made many drawings of ballet dancers practising at the barre. As an aide-mémoire he inscribed most of these drawings with information about the ballet pose the dancer is holding. His inscription can be seen here in the top left corner, recording that the dancer, on points, is practising the second position. Occasionally his inscriptions contain critical comments about the dancer's position – for example bad legs or arms. Did Degas himself struggle with capturing the dancer's pose? In this drawing we see that he has made various attempts at establishing the placing of her right arm.

Here he brilliantly conveys the fullness of the dancer's romantic tutu and her erect stance against the horizontal of the barre, the hasty shading establishing her distance from the wall itself. There are just some notes of pink for her slippers and right arm, touches of yellow on her waist and left elbow, and gouache highlighting the contour of the calf of her lower right leg and a splash on her cheek and chin.

Degas usually kept drawings like this in a portfolio and would return to them later, either for ideas or for checking the details of a particular ballet position. These are not the sort of works he would have considered exhibiting or selling. This one, however, has been signed and inscribed 'à mon ami Fourcaud' (to my friend Fourcaud). It is very likely that Fourcaud was given the drawing as a gift during a visit to Degas's studio.

Louis de Fourcaud, a prolific author, journalist and art and music critic, was an important early supporter of the Impressionists and was particularly close to Edouard Manet and Pierre-Auguste Renoir. He had studied the cello at the Conservatoire de Paris and as a critic was doubtless an *abonné* (subscriber) to the Opéra. VH

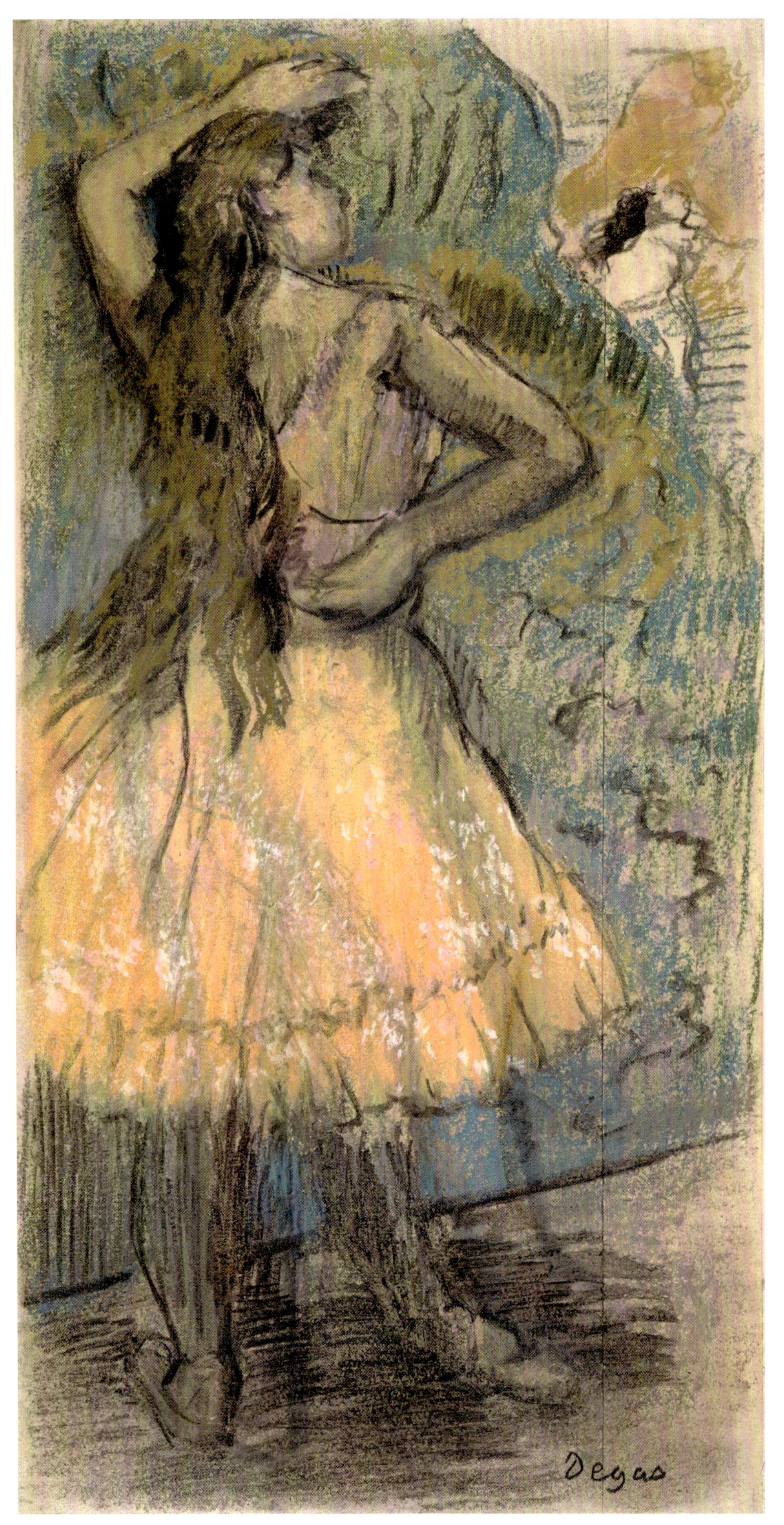
Degas

16 *Dancer*

About 1888
Pastel on tracing paper
45 × 23 cm
The Burrell Collection, Glasgow
35.230

In this small and vibrant pastel a dancer leans against a piece of stage scenery, probably slightly off-stage to the left. Her seeming tiredness suggests she has already performed and now waits her turn to dance once more. Her left arm, leaning against the scenery, is held high above her head, while her right arm stretches out from her body, her hand resting just behind her waist. Both arms form triangles that mirror each other, and her legs and feet echo the position of her arms. Similarly, the shape of her tutu is echoed in the shape of her upper body. Degas, as ever, is more interested in exploring form and space than in capturing a dancer posed in a natural position.

We can make out Degas's constant changes, first sketching in the bare legs of his dancer and then adding strokes of green and orange pastel and the firm charcoal outline of her tutu. Dissatisfied with the resulting area of this thin vertical paper, he has had a piece of paper added, extending the right edge further towards the stage itself.

This is one of a series of drawings and pastels in which Degas included a figure in this pose. Sometimes, as here, the figure is alone, while in other works two or more dancers are present. Rather than drawing from a model or even from something he has seen, Degas worked from his own earlier drawings using a process of transfer and replication, with the same pose appearing again and again, sometimes facing in one direction and sometimes another. In the later years of his career this repetition of particular poses became an obsession, with Degas experimenting with a stock of motifs that he repeated, modified or transposed from one composition to the next.

We know that Degas considered *Dancer* a finished work of art because he has signed it, something he only did when it was to be exhibited or had found a purchaser.

William Burrell bought this pastel from the London dealer Wallis & Son on 28 May 1928 for £392. VH

17 *Three Dancers*

About 1900–5
Pastel on tracing paper
50.8 × 47 cm
The Burrell Collection, Glasgow
35.249

During the last years of his painting career, Degas rarely worked on a unique representation of a particular subject. Like *The Red Ballet Skirts* (cat. 19), this pastel is one of a 'series' in which he explored similar groupings of figures, experimenting with different colour harmonies in each work. There are at least ten pastels, in collections all over the world, that relate directly to *Three Dancers*. It has been suggested that Degas intended to exhibit these works as a 'suite', just as Monet had shown several 'series' of pictures at Durand-Ruel's gallery, including one in 1904. The possibility that Degas was under pressure from dealers to produce 'finished' works at this time has also been proposed.

The dancers wait among the stage-flats, a '*décor d'arbres*'. The dancer in the foreground, her hands on her hips, is stretching her upper body. All three dancers look intently in the same direction, no doubt watching the performance on stage, awaiting their next entrance.

In these late works Degas improvises with a charcoal 'armature' and a stunning series of colour symphonies, the pastel sometimes only lightly scratching the paper and at others superimposing dense webs of striated pigment. He rarely signed these late works and so it is an indication of its importance that this work is signed – and not once, but twice. The signature tells us that Degas considered the work finished. VH

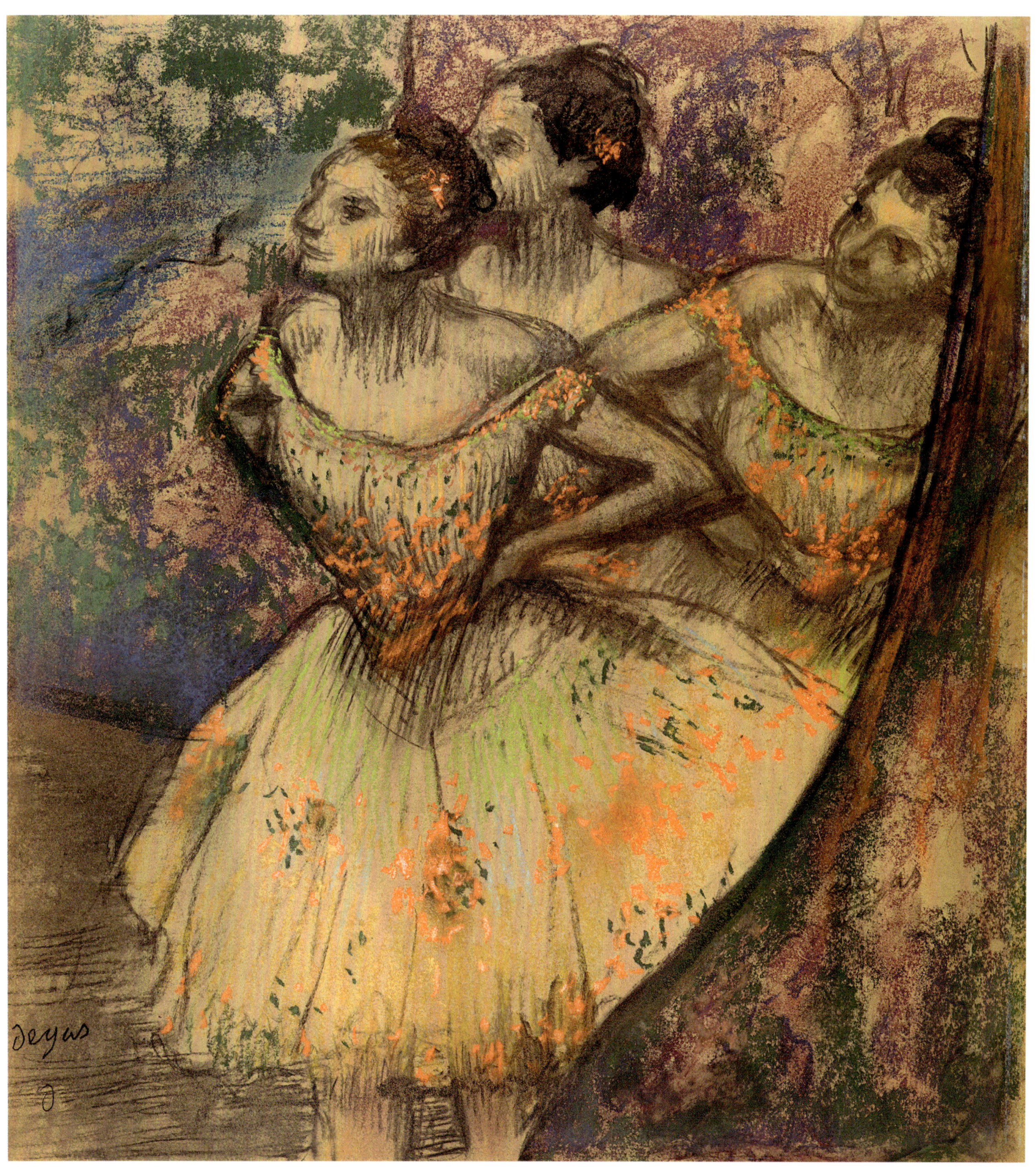
Degas

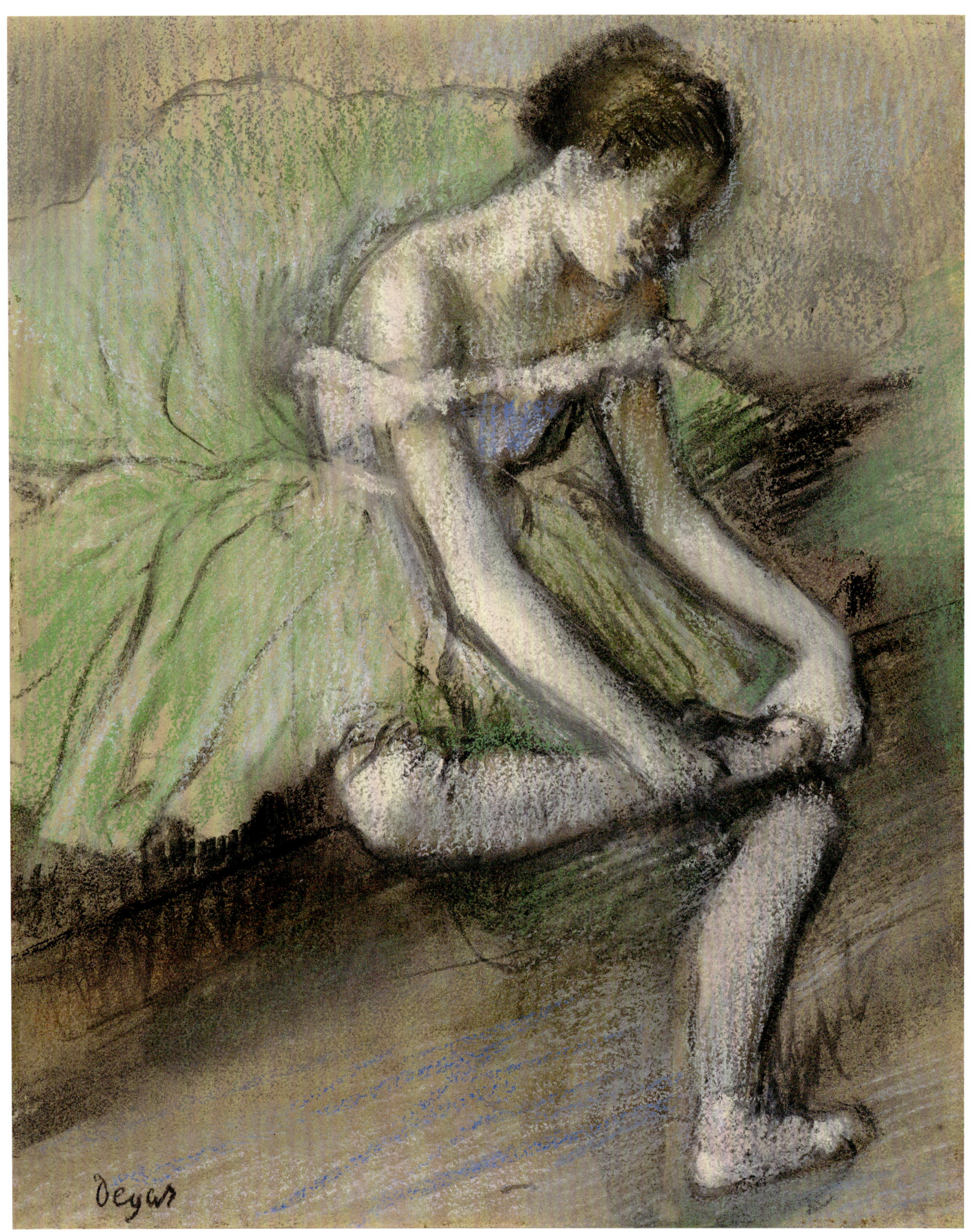
Degas

18 *The Green Ballet Skirt*

About 1896
Pastel on tracing paper
45 × 37 cm
The Burrell Collection, Glasgow
35.242

In this late pastel a ballet dancer rests, her right, slipper-clad foot clasped in her hand as she supports and massages her aching limb.

Like many of Degas's late works, *The Green Ballet Skirt* is executed in charcoal and pastel on tracing paper, which he has had laid down on board. The quick, jagged strokes of sky blue in the dancer's bodice are repeated as long strokes of unexplained blue on the wooden floorboards. Degas has superimposed layers of charcoal over the soft tints of flesh colour on her left arm. Pentimenti are clearly visible where he has changed his mind about the placing of her right knee and left ankle. Yet he was obviously happy with this work and considered it finished, as it bears his signature.

Throughout his career Degas repeated and revised poses that particularly interested him. This practice became more frequent in the 1890s, which explains why we see the same poses or motifs occurring and recurring in different works. He used two methods to facilitate this: he would trace a drawing or make a counter-proof. To make a counter-proof he would moisten a sheet of paper and press it onto an existing drawing in charcoal or pastel. The new sheet would now bear a faint, reversed impression of the original drawing. Degas could then work up this new drawing, experimenting by working in pastels of different colours or by combining the original pose or motif with new motifs. He could revise the image by expanding it, adding extra sheets of paper, or by cropping it.

This constant exploring and experimenting is surely a sign of his genius. Degas was never happy until he had tried innumerable combinations of the glorious colours available to him, and many intricate forms, as he sought after a new vision. VH

19 *The Red Ballet Skirts*

About 1900
Pastel on tracing paper
76.8 × 57.8 cm
The Burrell Collection, Glasgow
35.243

In this late pastel three dancers are seen waiting in the wings during a performance. They are no longer the elegant, sylph-like figures performing graceful movements under bright lights, but are heavy, awkward and tired. Against a backdrop of a stage flat, we see them resting and stretching or arching their weary backs.

Throughout his career Degas seems to have preferred showing ballet dancers off stage. While allowing him to depict the dancers in their vibrant stage costumes, it meant he could explore the expressive poses and gestures of their spontaneous, natural movements, rather than the repeated and learned, rehearsed movements of the ballet.

This is not a unique work in that it is one in a 'series' of near-identical variants of a composition that seems to have obsessed Degas. Many charcoal drawings and some ten pastels relate to it directly. One of his models, Pauline, recorded Degas working on these late pastels. She describes how the artist painted the same subject over and over again, but each time using different colours and tones – variations in yellow, blue, green – until one of the pastels pleased him enough for him to consider it finished. The others in the series, like *The Red Ballet Skirts*, were left more or less unfinished.

The dancers in the Burrell pastel wear glowing orange-red 'romantic' tutus against a green background. In a similar work, today in a private collection, he reversed this colour balance. In another, now in the Cincinnati Art Museum, the dancers wear lemon tutus against a deep Prussian blue ground. Of the group of pastels relating to *The Red Ballet Skirts*, only one work was signed and sold during Degas's lifetime. VH

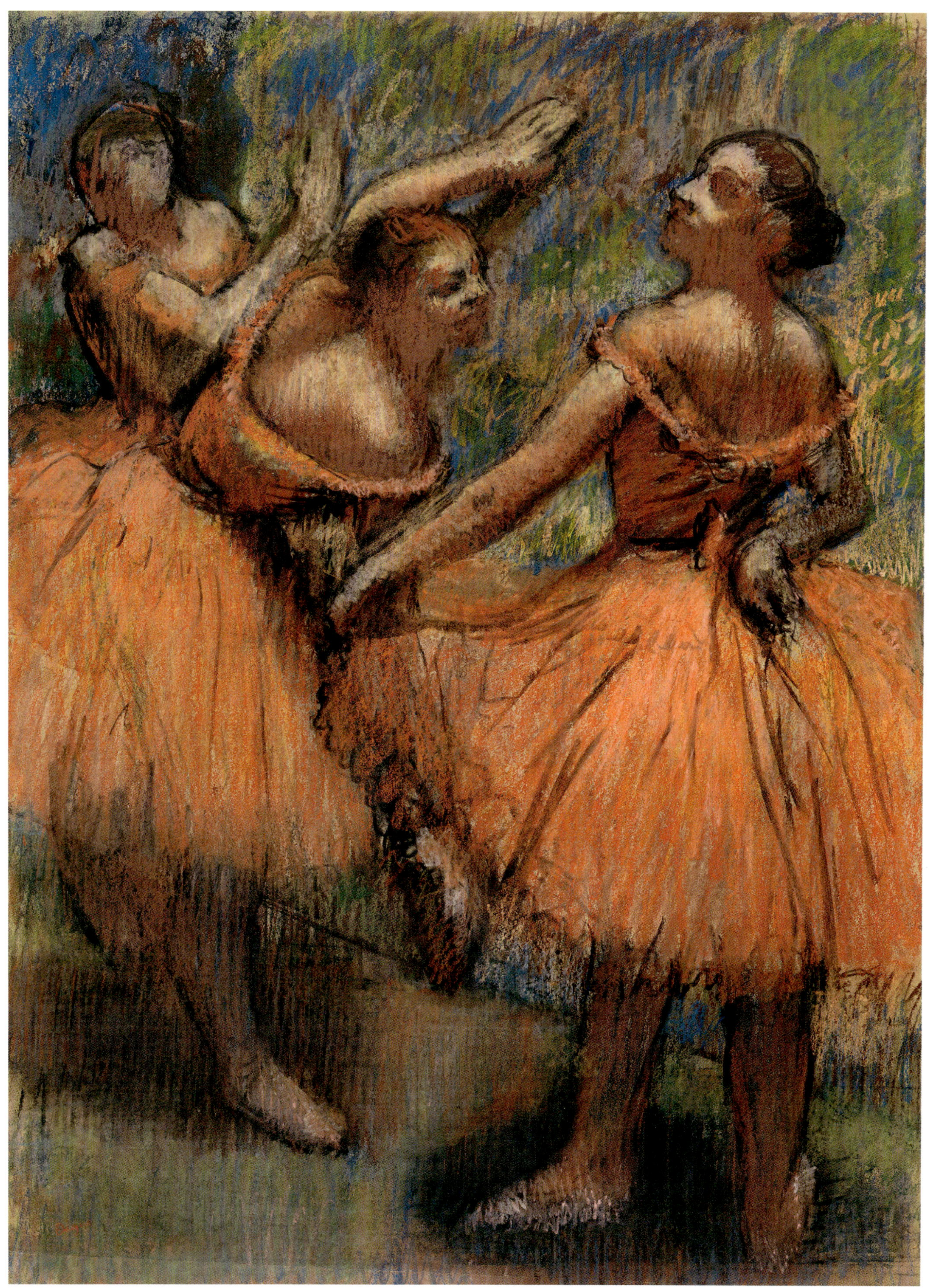

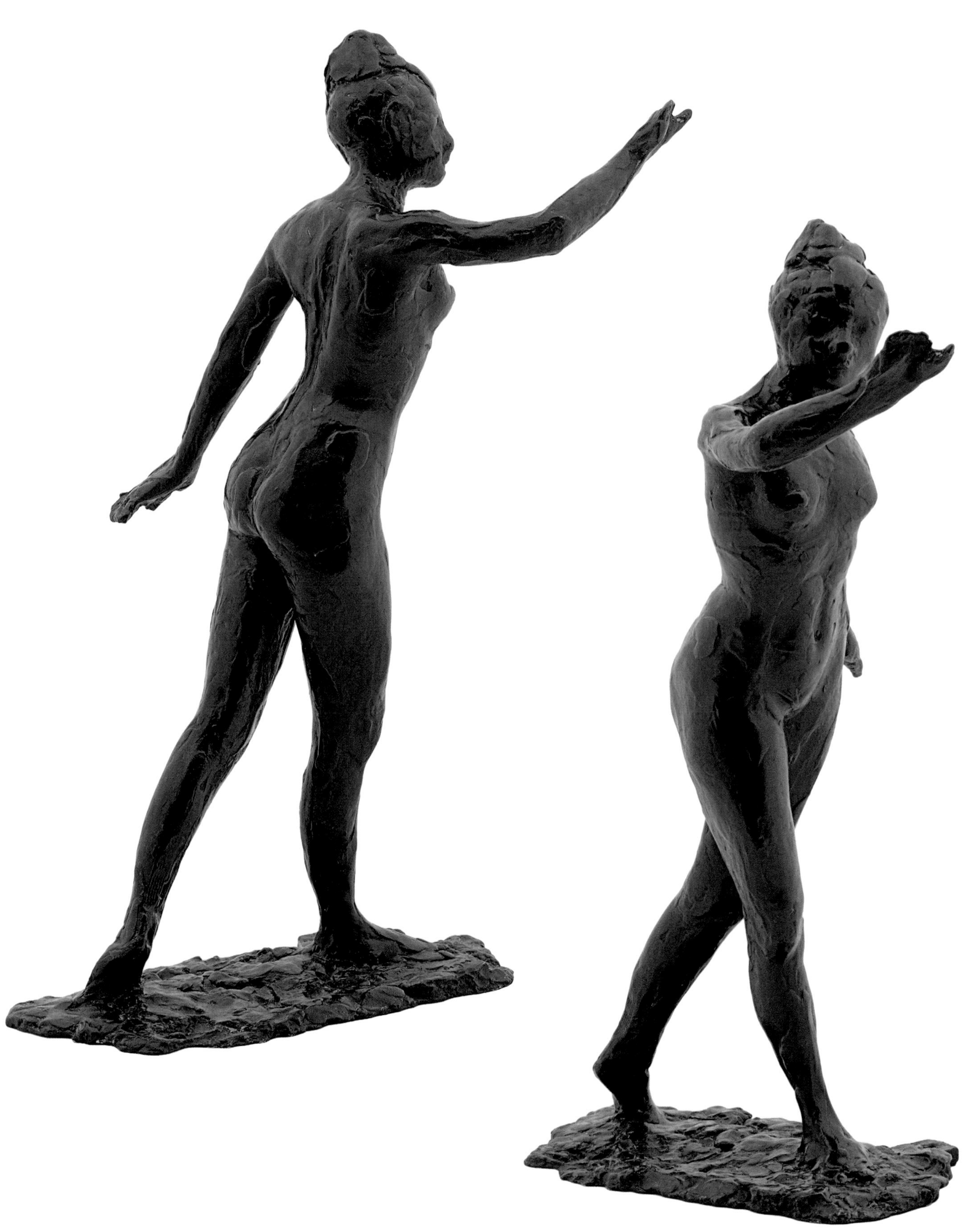

20 *Grande Arabesque, First Time*

About 1885–90, posthumous cast
Bronze
48.5 × 23 cm
Kelvingrove Art Gallery and Museum, Glasgow, given by Messrs Alex. Reid and Lefevre Ltd, 1952
S.267

It was probably in the 1860s that Degas began to experiment with making sculptures out of wax, clay and Plastiline (modelling clay). His favoured subjects were those he had already explored in other media: horses, dancers and women at their toilette. Famously difficult to pose for, as his eyesight failed in later life he would have to feel with his hands the model he could not always see.

During his lifetime Degas showed only one wax, *The Little Dancer* at the Sixth Impressionist Exhibition in 1881. The vast majority of his sculptures were cast in bronze only after his death. It is thought that he made them simply for his personal use, that he viewed them as ephemera which would eventually disintegrate of their own accord. He claimed that 'the only reason that I made wax figures of animals and humans was for my own satisfaction … in order to give my paintings and drawings greater expression, greater ardour and more life. They are exercises to get me going; documentary, preparatory motions, nothing more…'.

With her weight on her right leg, the dancer's left leg is extended to the back, echoed in her gently lifted arm and gracefully tilted hand. Her right arm is raised high in front. The pose is related to two others: *Grande Arabesque, Second Time (Arabesque on the Right)* and *Grande Arabesque, Third Time (First Arabesque Penchée)*, the waxes for which are in the National Gallery of Art, Washington. Indeed, despite the differing arms of this figure, some scholars see them as each representing a phase in one arabesque, the dancer gradually bending her body while simultaneously lifting her leg high into the air, a sculptural equivalent of the photographs of figures in motion of Eadweard Muybridge (1830–1904) and Etienne-Jules Marey (1830–1904). SH

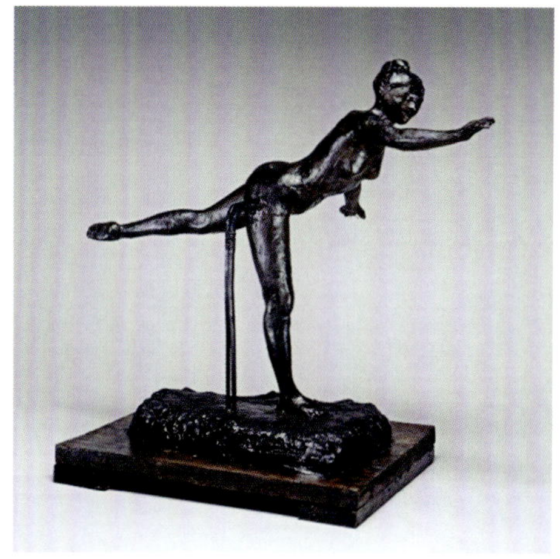

Fig. 18
Edgar Degas (1834–1917)
Grande Arabesque, Second Time (Arabesque on the Right), about 1885–90
Pigmented beeswax, clay, metal armature, cork, on wooden base,
48.1 × 56.4 × 21.7 cm
National Gallery of Art, Washington, DC
1999.80.9

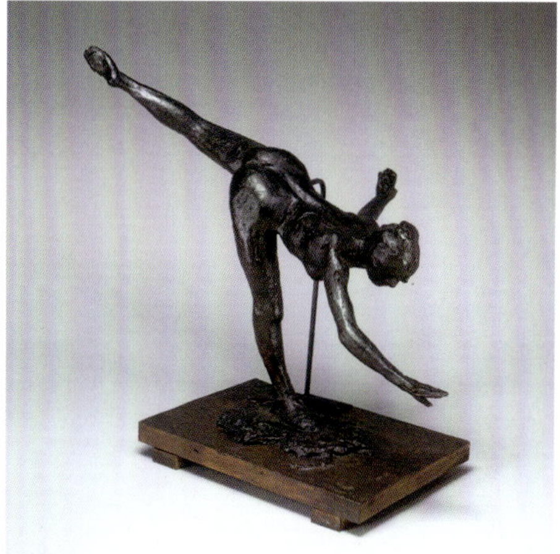

Fig. 19
Edgar Degas (1834–1917)
Grande Arabesque, Third Time (First Arabesque Penchée), about 1885–90
Pigmented beeswax, clay, metal armature, cork, on wooden base,
42 × 55.5 × 31.8 cm
National Gallery of Art, Washington, DC
1999.80.10

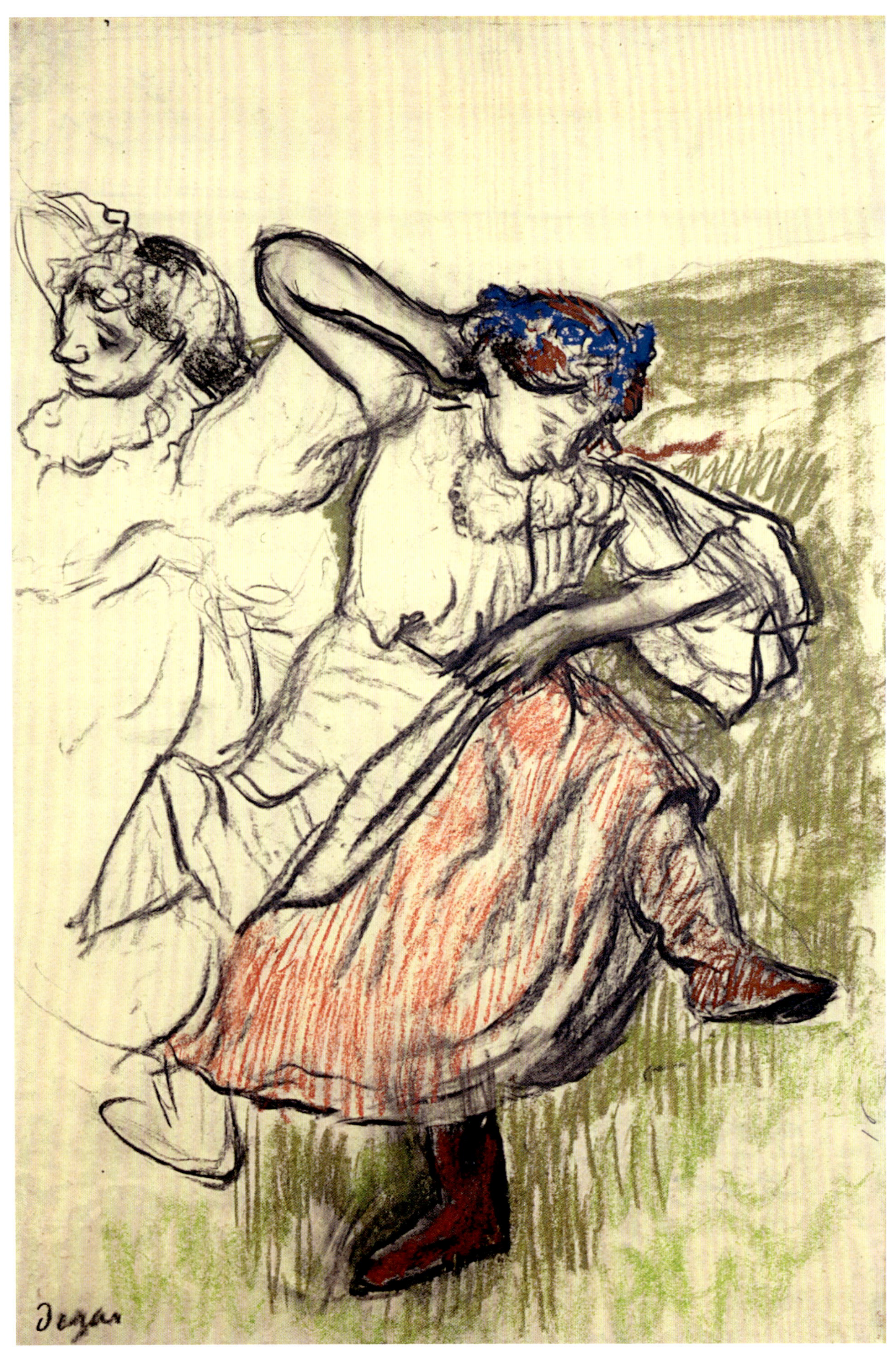
Degas

21 *Russian Dancers*

About 1899
Charcoal and pastel on tracing paper
65 × 44.5 cm
Berwick-upon-Tweed Museum & Art Gallery

Arm raised to back of head, a Russian dancer kicks her booted left foot and with her left hand lifts an overskirt or apron to allow her long, thick peasant skirt to participate in the ecstatic movement. Degas was intent on capturing a single figure isolated from her dancing companions in what was a complicated new experience of movement for him, full of primitive energy. At left, Degas sketches the same head in reverse. Both look down, to the earth and to their feet, alive only to the pounding music and indifferent to the observer in a way a ballet dancer, trained in addressing herself to her audience while appearing indifferent to it, never is.

Tracing paper, used here, is translucent. It allowed for figures to be traced later on, and traced in reverse as well. The principal figure here, for example, appears in several of Degas's multi-figure Russian Dancer compositions. The central figure in cat. 22 is her exact reverse; there, the dancer is partially overlapped by a companion, seen from the rear. Having observed and sketched several of the most distinctive movements of the Russian dancers, Degas felt free to combine individual figures in increasingly complicated and colourful compositions. But the starting point for him always seems to have been the single figure.

Colour too seems to have been secondary in the process of elaborating his compositions. If he called some of his more elaborate Russian Dancer compositions 'veritable orgies of colour', he must have referred to works relatively late in the gestation of his compositions. A sheet like this, for example, is essentially an energetic charcoal drawing. A few deft touches of pastel in the red skirt, and brilliant blue above suggesting ribbons and flowers in the hair, hint at how the artist might have developed colouristic intensity. Instead he stopped, in order, it seems, to sharply reinforce with charcoal the principal lines of force in the composition, including the dancer's arms and the hems of her clothes. The background is partially brushed in with vertical lines of green pastel in order to suggest the ambient space in which the dancer moves. Is it a stage set evoking the Russian steppes? Unlike his ballet paintings, where Degas often took pains to establish that we are observing something highly artificial, a production on stage, here he leaves our reading of that space ambiguous. It could be that we are seeing these peasant women dancing out-of-doors, in nature itself.

This was one of numerous works that William Burrell donated to the museum in Berwick-upon-Tweed in 1949. CR

22 *Russian Dancers*

About 1899
Pastel and charcoal on tracing paper
73 × 59.1 cm
The National Gallery, London
NG 6581

Degas rarely showed works in progress but on 1 July 1899 he made a point of taking Julie Manet, the daughter of his late friend the painter Berthe Morisot (1841–1895), up to his studio to see three pastels of dancers in Russian costumes, their hair garlanded with flowers. The entry in Julie Manet's diary is the one sure date establishing when, late in his career, Degas was at work on these vibrant pastels in which dancers, who are probably Ukrainian rather than Russian in origin, form complicated, interweaving patterns as they stomp the ground and kick out their legs, shod in high red boots. The date in the late 1890s corresponds broadly to known visits to Paris by such exotic troupes from Eastern Europe.

Most such works are, as here, on tracing paper, and many of the poses are repeated from sheet to sheet, or indeed repeated in reverse. Degas studied individual poses in large preliminary charcoal drawings sparingly touched with pastel. Conceivably, he traced a pose from one sheet to another, overlapping it with another pose from another sheet in various permutations of the dancers' most distinctive movements. The most prominent pose here with left hand to back of head is the reverse of the pose of the principal figure in cat. 21. Here, a strip of tracing paper has been added to the bottom of the sheet, extending the leg of the foremost dancer, seen from the rear, so that she almost seems to share the viewer's space. The exact pose of that dancer is then repeated a second time, behind the central figure as well as in front of her.

This is another of Degas's 'orgies of colour'. The pastel is densely applied in myriad hues and the sense of frenzy and of noisy, rushed movement is palpable. Indeed, after painting classical ballet for decades, the Russian dancers must have appeared to Degas as the antitheses of ballerinas. Whereas the latter seek to float, the Russians pound the ground. While ballerinas emulate sprites and dress in ethereal tulle, the Russians are women of the earth clad in heavy folk costumes. The high artificiality of ballet, derived from refined courtly culture, is replaced by dances deriving from primitive, centuries-old peasant customs. Here was a new kind of movement from a distant world and briefly, in an explosion of renewed creativity, Degas sought to capture its thrilling essence. CR

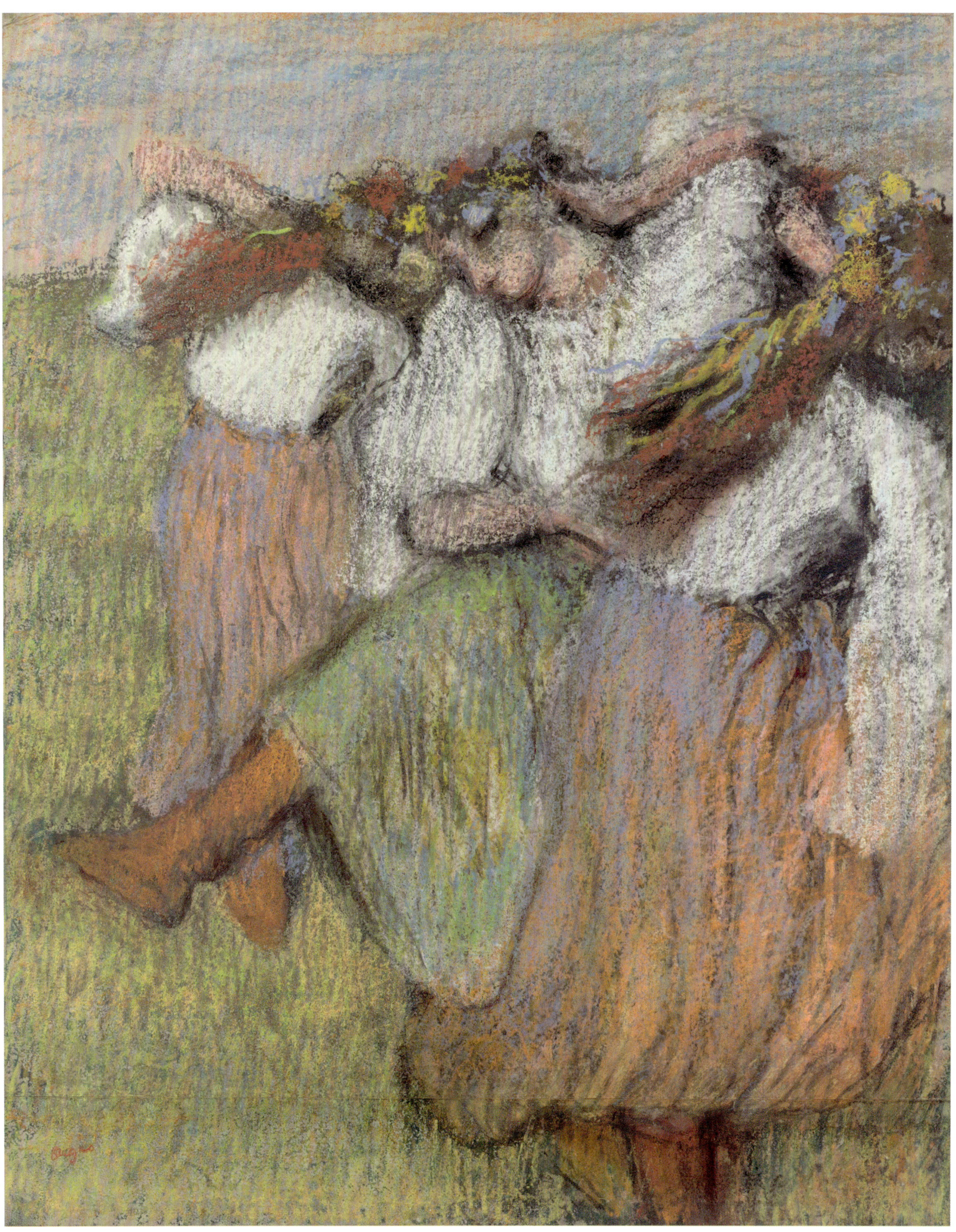

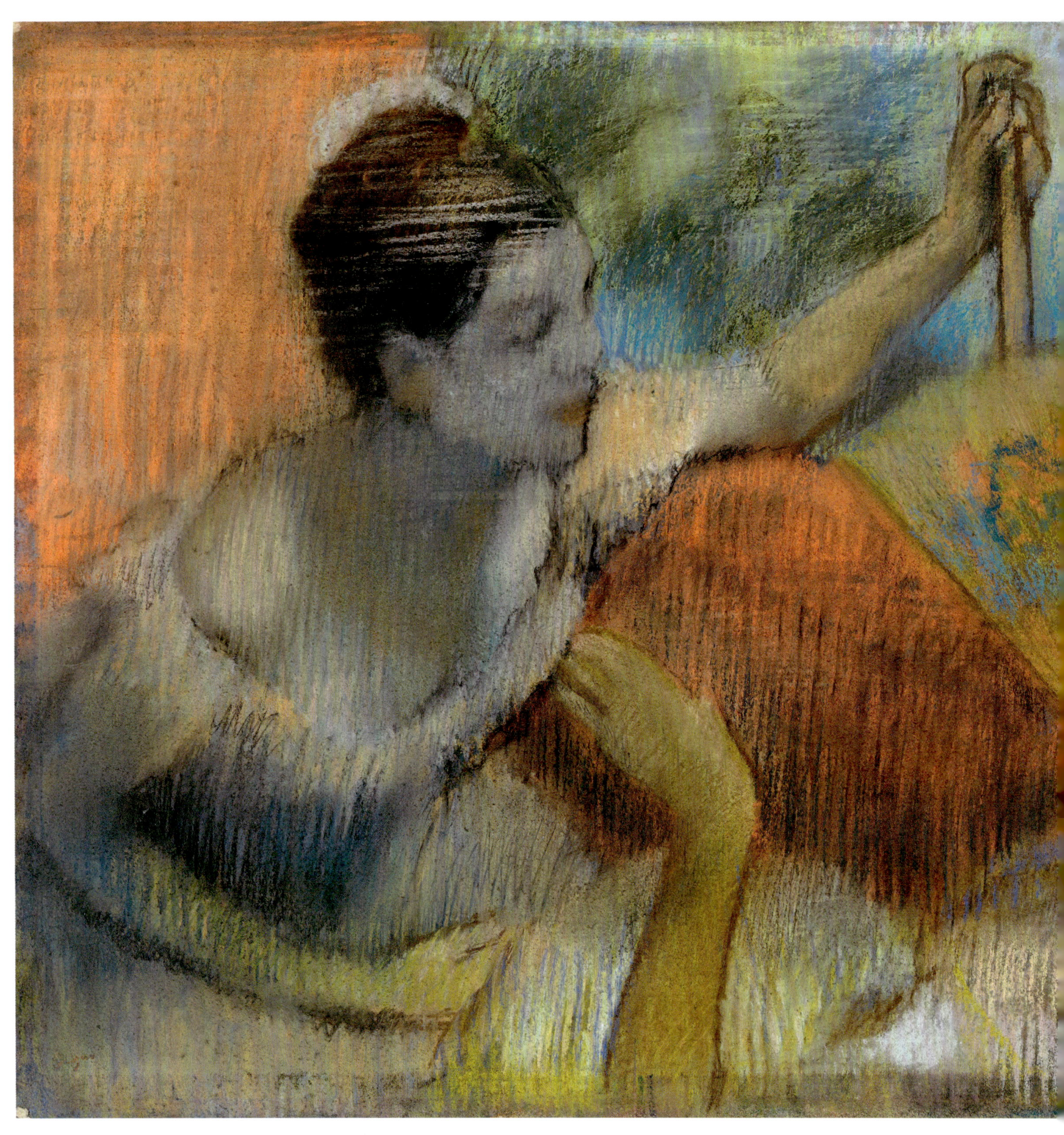

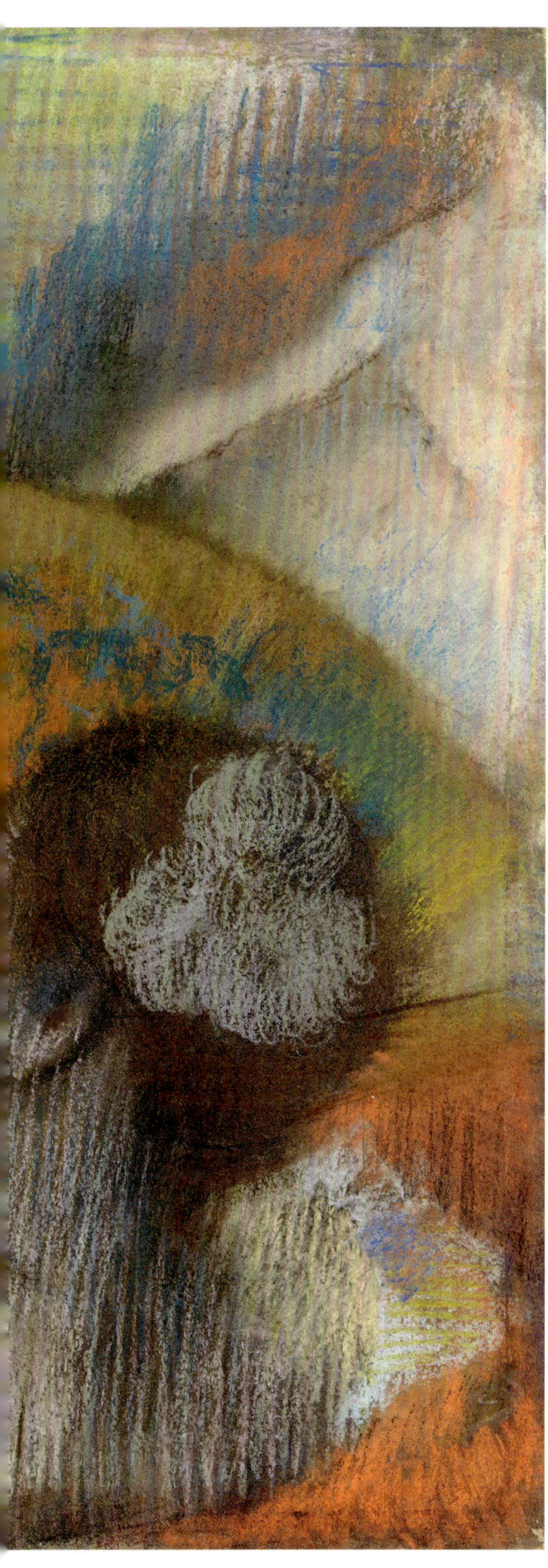

23 *Women in a Theatre Box*

About 1885–90
Pastel on paper
62.2 × 87 cm
The Burrell Collection, Glasgow
35.231

This is one of a number of drawings, pastels and prints on the theme of women in a theatre box overlooking a stage. In the other works the women with their jewels, fans and binoculars concentrate on the performance taking place below them. Here, two young women, shoulders bare, their hair pulled tightly back, are seated in the box, animatedly talking to each other and ignoring the performance. While the one on the left turns away from the stage to listen to her friend, her companion cannot even see the stage because her fan is shielding it from her view. The woman on the left rests her left elbow and her closed fan, held vertically, on the deep red and orange of the plush velvet box. Degas's very deliberate drawing of her hand is reminiscent of studies he made of the ballet master Perrot leaning on his stick: he no doubt lifted the motif from his studies of Perrot.

Degas has chosen a high viewpoint, allowing us to glimpse what is happening on the stage below: we can just make out a dancer in the spotlight in the top right corner. Are these two dancers themselves or are they wealthy society women? While it was highly unlikely that dancers would be allowed to watch a performance from a box, it was equally unlikely that society women would behave in the indecorous manner suggested here.

Some of Degas's contemporaries, such as Mary Cassatt and Pierre-Auguste Renoir, also painted young women attending theatre performances. Their paintings differ from those of Degas in that they chose to paint views of the young women from outside the *loge* looking in, either from below or from another box to the side. Only Degas places us inside the box, looking over the stage.

This pastel has a wonderfully dense textured surface. Degas uses a wide variety of techniques to achieve this richness: bold, strong, cross-hatchings suggest the strong greens and blues of the stage scenery. He animates and lightens this vibrant area by taking a sharp point, possibly the end of a brush, to make vertical striations through the pastel. VH

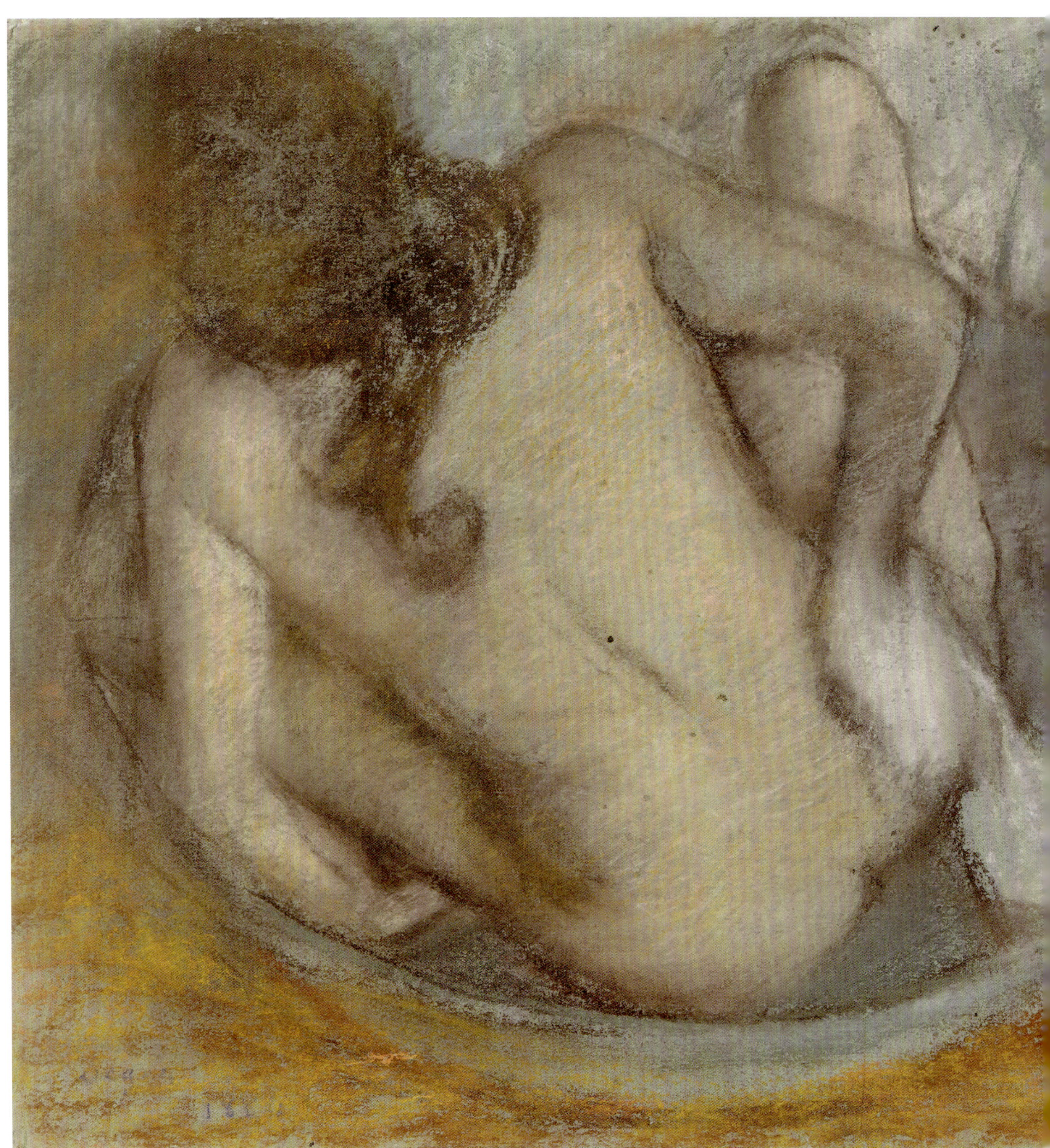

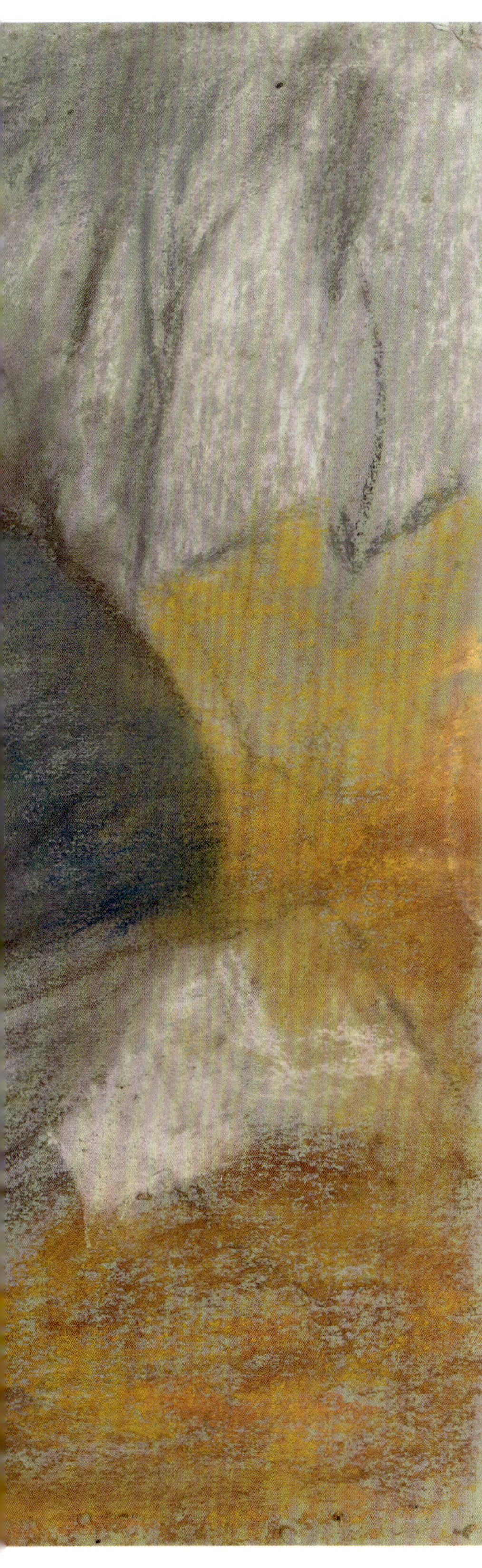

24 *Woman in a Tub*

1884
Pastel on paper
71.9 × 89.3 cm
The Burrell Collection, Glasgow
35.235
Not exhibited

Degas tackled traditional subjects in new ways. A woman bathing had been a frequent subject in Western European art – but usually the woman was represented as Venus, Diana or a classical nymph. Degas's bathers, like those of Courbet and Manet, were undoubtedly modern women. This pastel, which shows a woman bathing in a shallow metal tub, was one of a series of ten that Degas included in the Eighth (and last) Impressionist Exhibition in 1886. Of these women bathing, washing, drying themselves, doing their hair or having their hair done, we know from the many descriptive critical reviews that Burrell's work was number 25 in the catalogue (which included work by other artists) .

Degas's high viewpoint, while giving his work a sense of immediacy and originality, also helped distance him from his subject. As in many of his pastels, there are numerous pentimenti – literally, changes of mind. He uses dark contouring lines to describe the woman's form but there are different positions for all her limbs. An early line, cutting across from her right shoulder to her right elbow, reveals that her right arm was originally lower down. Degas has deliberately altered the contour of this arm to coincide with, and to continue, the curve of the tub. He could have made an attempt to hide these pentimenti but often he does not, allowing them to become part of the surface pattern of the pastel, themselves suggestive of movement and change. Similarly, he does not always alter the rest of the woman's form to take account of changes he has made. An example of this is clearly seen here in the woman's right leg. Her heavy and wide thigh is suddenly and unrealistically reduced at her knee.

How was this group of modern nudes received by the critics of the time? Interestingly, most avoided a discussion of meaning. Instead they praised the virtuosity of Degas's draughtsmanship and admired his having experimented with the pose and positioning of the women's bodies. The critic Mirbeau wrote of 'the terrifying sense of women under torture, of anatomies twisted and deformed by the violent contortions to which they are submitted'. Others found the pastels rather dark and monotone, complaining of the 'heavy, smoky tonality' that can certainly be seen here. Only a few voiced alarm at Degas's choice of subject, one finding them 'in perfect bad taste and totally lacking artistic qualities', another complaining of 'the subject's rather excessive intimacy'. VH

25 *Woman in a Tub*

About 1896–1901
Pastel on paper
60.8 × 84.6 cm
The Burrell Collection, Glasgow
35.236

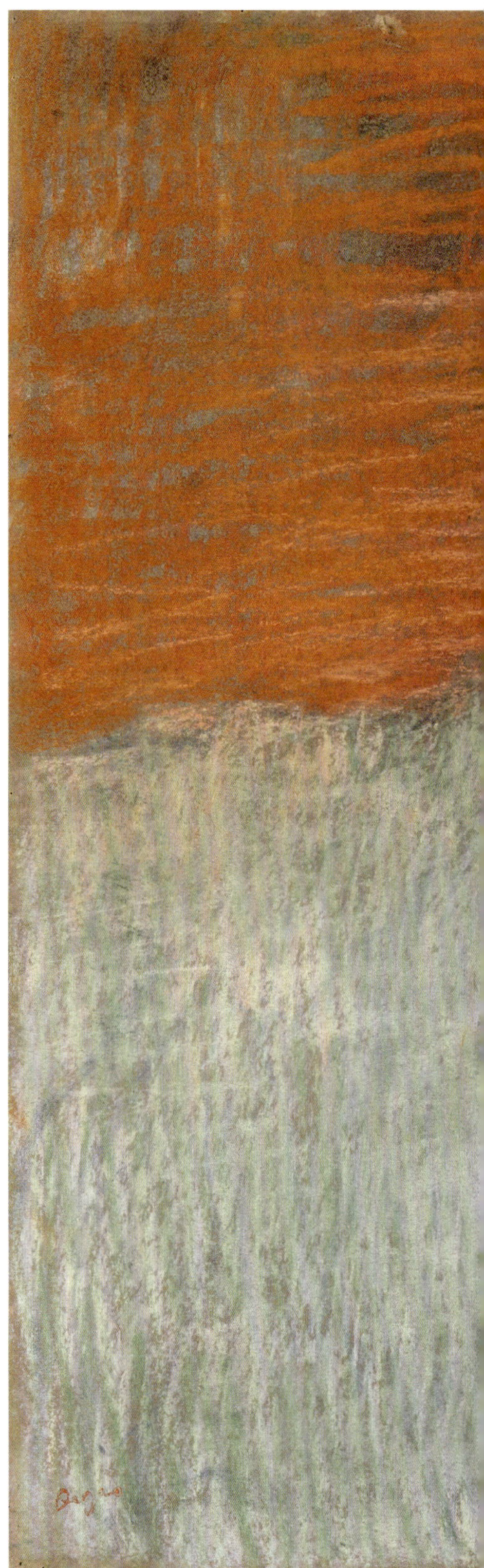

In this striking horizontal-format pastel Degas depicts a woman about to bathe with the sponge she holds in her right hand. She is standing in a shallow metal tub whose blue tones contrast with the vibrant orange background.

This rather awkward, angular nude is based on bathers that Degas painted much earlier, in the mid-1880s. Although he reused an earlier pose, did he refer back to the earlier works, would he have worked from memory or would he have had a model pose for him? It is difficult to know. While late in life Degas was fond of saying that a good artist should be capable of working from memory, there is plenty of evidence, from his friends and his models, to show that he worked from life right up until the end of his career.

If in the 1880s Degas's pastels remained essentially faithful to local colour, by the following decade, as can be seen here, he was increasingly using exaggerated, and not necessarily realistic, colour combinations. Here he has used strong directional strokes of bold colour – blue, green, orange, pink, white – which have been laid over heavily worked, darker ground colours. He began by delineating the contours of the woman's body with dark lines, and then used hatched strokes of mint green and pink to establish the flesh tone. Quick, jagged strokes of orange and yellow suggest the form of the woman's right breast and equally hasty strokes of yellow imply the form of her right thigh. The woman's surroundings are blocked in in confident, bold areas, forming square and rectangular forms that contrast with the shape of the oval tub.

Contemporary critics admired Degas's nudes for their realism, for his accurate observation of the imperfections of the flesh, finding them truthful, unlike the 'whitened, pinkened, soufflé-like flesh of [the] academic formula' they so despised. The critic Geffroy insisted that Degas's nudes represented 'a real naked woman' expressed with 'sincerity and truth'. Yet the critics also wrote about the abstract qualities of these nudes. In this pastel Degas's rich, tactile handling, bold colouring, geometric forms, his use of space and lack of narrative detail, and his experimentation with the woman's pose could indeed lead us to conclude that the subject itself has almost disappeared. VH

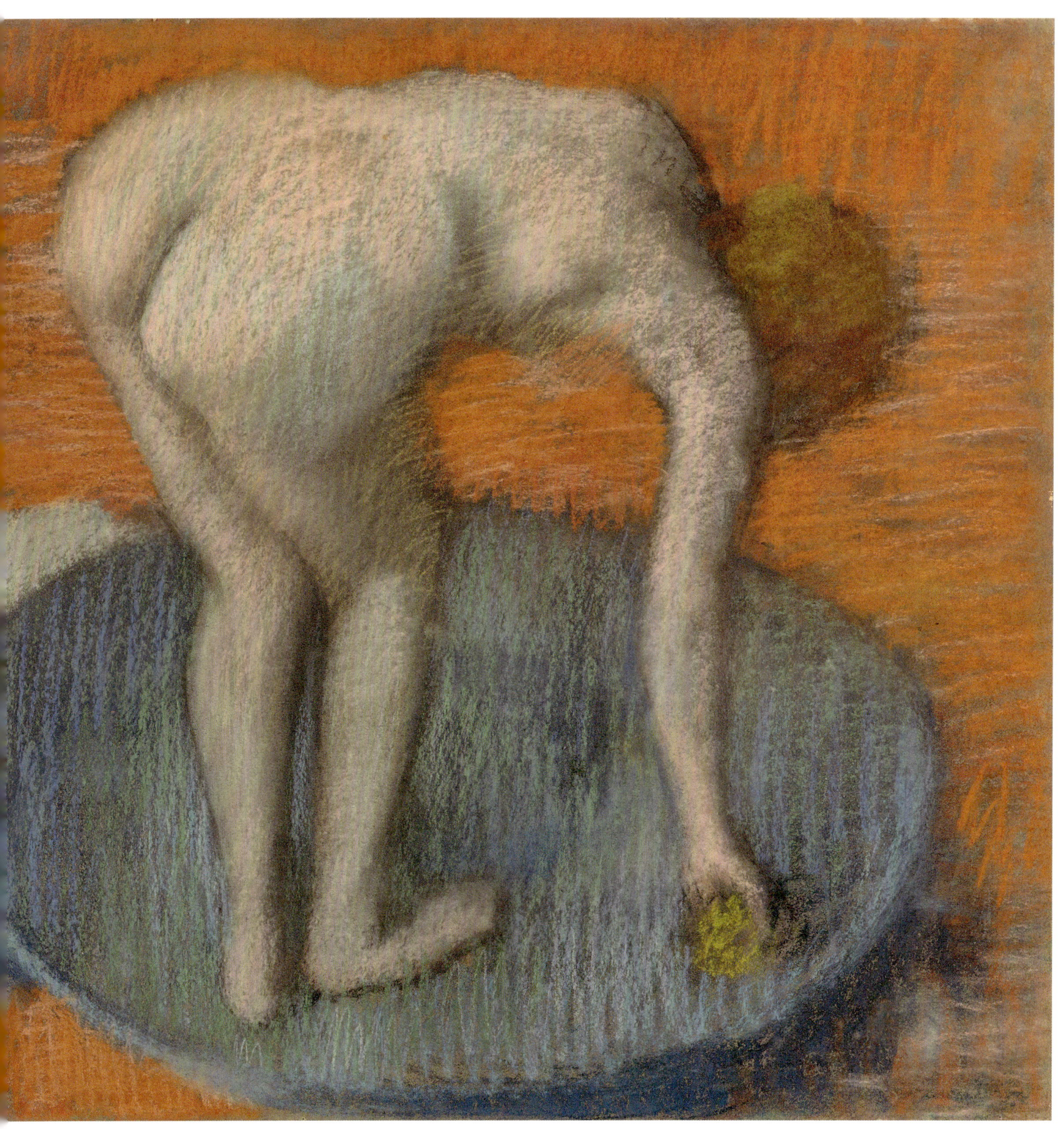

26 *After the Bath*

About 1896
Oil on canvas
74.9 × 81.3 cm
The National Gallery, London. Bequeathed by Simon Sainsbury 2006

In the final phase of his career Degas delighted in studying models positioned in increasingly complicated poses, some almost painfully contorted. This bather is no exception. Having just come out of the bathtub in the background, a naked woman dries herself, propped up on a chaise longue, her body sprawling diagonally across the entire composition. The pose has been described as a poignant blend of eroticism and anguish and is characteristic of the complexity of Degas's art, finding undeniable beauty in a twisted and uncomfortable pose.

This painting is one of three related oils all entitled *After the Bath* and executed around 1896. The genesis of this series is unclear as two pastel and charcoal drawings, both also dated 1896, seem to have served to establish the pose of the three paintings, as also does a gelatin silver print of the same date (fig. 5, p. 18), thought to be Degas's only recorded photograph of a bather. While it is impossible to establish whether he first carefully posed his model for the photograph and then proceeded with the drawings, or whether he produced the photograph in imitation of this composition, the three paintings that followed offer different responses to these initial studies.

In this oil painting, in a similar fashion to the photograph, the bather's sensuality is emphasised by subtle gradations of tone along her spine following the shadows cast by the contours of her skin. All the elements of the work are infused with a tactile sensuality: even the sponge in the foreground emphasises the bather's supple naked body. The blurred outlines and the overall softness of the colours Degas achieved in oil resemble the aesthetic of pastel, and could also hint at the photograph, suggesting the fluidity he was able to achieve among different media.

The two other versions of this subject are more pared down: one (private collection) is set in an unusual vertical format and locates the bather behind the bathtub, a gaping black hole in the foreground of the composition; the other (fig. 6, p. 18) is a more spontaneously painted monochromatic study in red, in which the bather occupies the right-hand two thirds of the composition, elevated as if on a pedestal, and much more autonomous from her surroundings. The present version is the smallest of the three related paintings, but is the most heavily worked and has the greatest visual complexity. JD

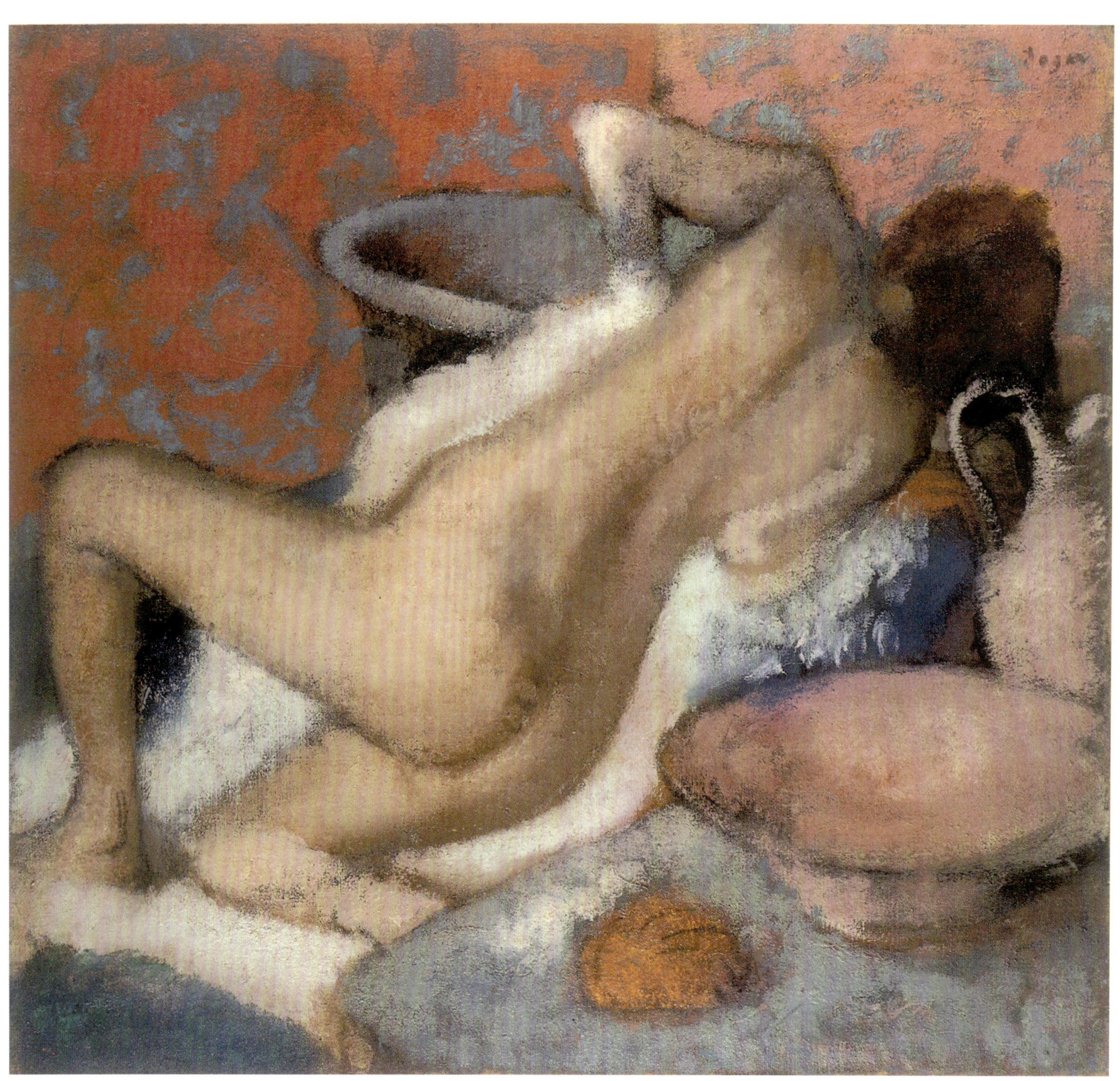
Degas

27 *After the Bath, Woman drying herself*

About 1890–5
Pastel on paper
103.5 × 98.5 cm
The National Gallery, London
NG 6295

In striking contrast to some of the preceding tormented nudes, this bather is comfortably seated on a low upholstered chair. Her yellow slipper and the thick patterned carpet of the bathroom imbue the image with an air of cosy domesticity. One hand on the bathtub, she steadies herself as she dries the nape of her neck with a thick and luxurious white towel, wrapped around her and the chair. She has the monumental presence of a classical figure, echoing Degas's own words regarding his series of bathers: 'to think that in another age I would have been painting Susanna and the Elders'.

Despite this air of serenity and tranquillity, Degas handled the pastel with great vigour and variety. Some areas, such as the towel next to the woman's red hair, were obtained by wetting the white pastel stick, while her back is constructed of overlapping areas of bold cross-hatchings. Degas left a significant number of pastel strokes unfixed in order to maximise the colours' brilliance: for instance, the extraordinary vertical strokes of violet in the shadows, and creamy white for the highlights of the woman's back, or the zigzags of fluorescent yellow over the orange back of the chair and dark blue to suggest shadows. In the brightest areas, such as the bather's arms, the highlights extend slightly beyond the figure's outline in order to suggest movement and the flickering play of light.

Degas began with a tightly composed study of the bather's back on a single sheet of paper and then expanded his composition in order to locate the figure in space, including more room for the fore- and background. This work is composed of seven sheets: two short horizontal strips at the top, two at the bottom and three larger strips down the middle. Degas would often re-size his pastels in this way, developing the core of the image, and then would take the work to his framer, usually Lézin on the rue Guénégaud, who would mount the sheet on a board and add extra pieces of paper, sometimes no more than a few millimetres wide, to enlarge the composition according to Degas's instructions. Degas probably started colouring the central sheet before extending the composition, hence the difference in colour density, for instance at the lower left, midway up the bather's shin, revealing the division between the initial sheet and the added sections. JD

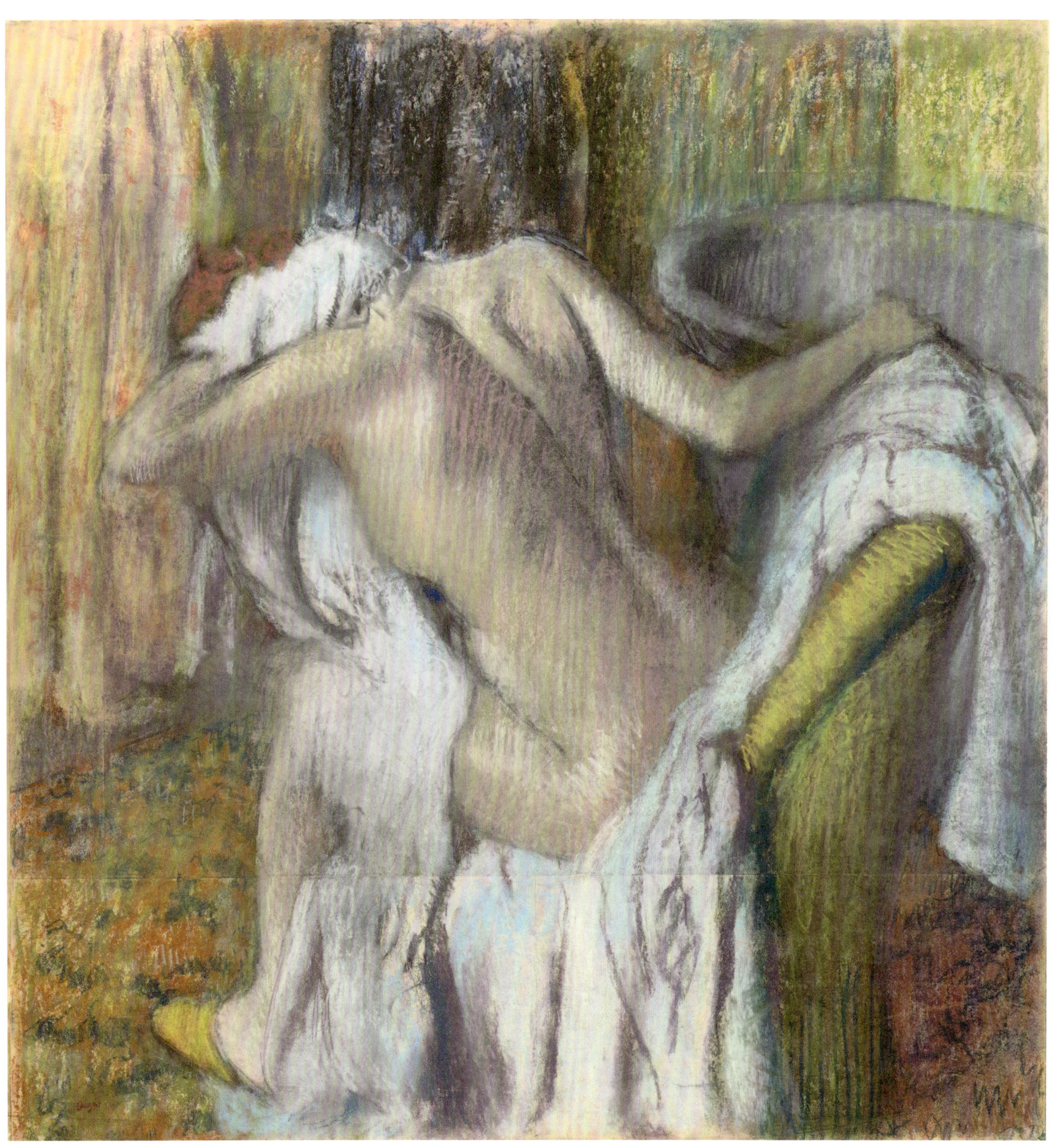

28 *After the Bath*

About 1890–5
Charcoal and pastel on paper
38 × 34 cm
The Burrell Collection, Glasgow
35.247

This charcoal and pastel drawing is a preparatory study Degas made in the last years of his life, when he was working on a sequence of lithographs of a bather drying her hip. Each of the lithographs shows a bather bending over, attended by a maidservant who holds a towel or a robe. It was to be the last printmaking enterprise of his life.

Degas has patched on three additional pieces of paper along the top, right and bottom edges of the drawing, as he often did. The additions have allowed him to include more of the bathing figure and to make sense of what she is doing with her left hand – sponging her hip rather than drying it. It has also allowed him to develop the floral wallpaper, something he then makes more of in the final lithograph.

In the final state of the lithograph Degas only leaves the maid's hands holding the towel so that its top edge makes a continuous line with the bather's shoulders. Unlike other versions of the maid in the prints, in this drawing her head and shoulders are prominent and her face looks blandly out to the right. Her strong, rather rigid bearing and her heavy face, short hair and the 'cylinder' of her neck have caused some to see in her echoes of a classical figure. VH

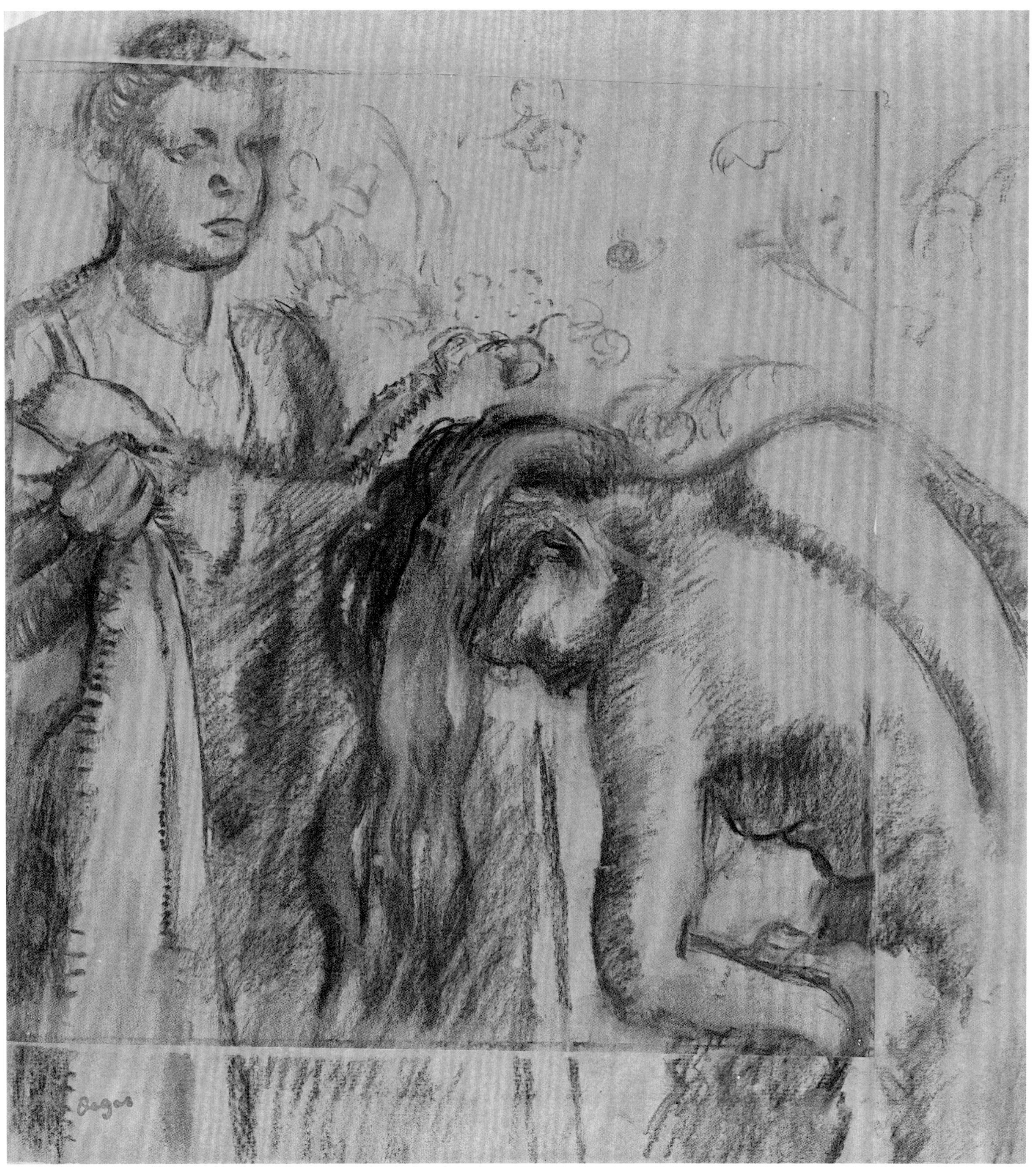
Degas

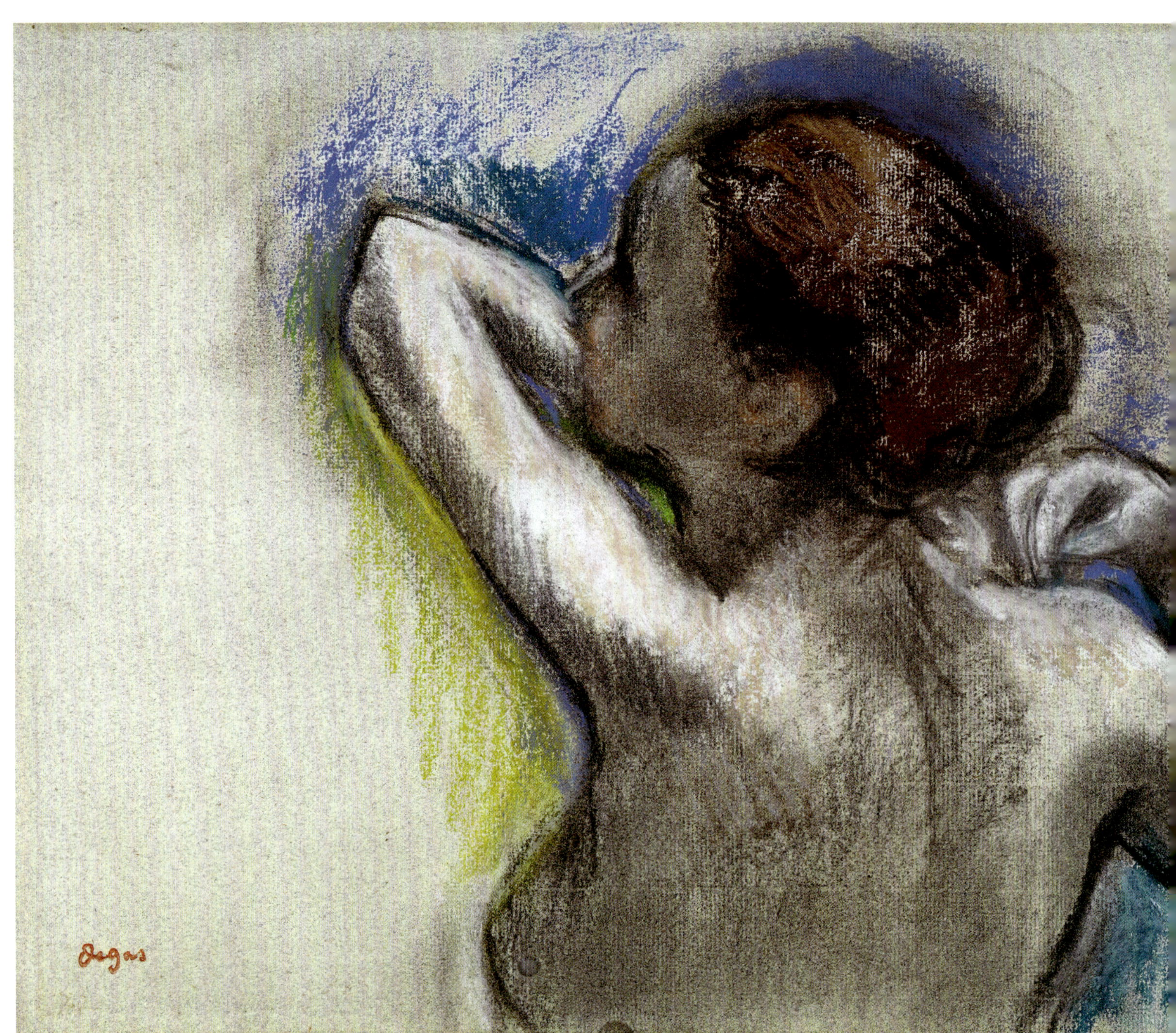
Degas

29 *Dancer adjusting her Shoulder Strap*

About 1896–9
Charcoal and pastel on paper
28 × 47 cm
The Burrell Collection, Glasgow
35.248

Although Degas is often classed as an Impressionist, his method of working was very different from that of Monet, Renoir, Pissarro or Sisley. While they chose to paint outside, working directly on to the canvas, Degas worked in his studio, building up his paintings and pastels from numerous drawings and studies.

This is one such study, of a dancer adjusting the strap of her dress (although here Degas has worked from a naked model), which in turn would be used in the creation of a finished pastel or painting. This was a motif that Degas used frequently. His early training and his study of antique sculpture inspired him with particular gestures and movements which he then made modern and his own. It has been suggested that it was one of his own sculptures that suggested this motif, and certainly the use of shading in the drawing gives relief to the figure.

This wonderfully elegant and striking study is full of movement and colour. The dancer, her chestnut brown hair tied up at her neck, stands with her back to us, her graceful left profile and her slender fame silhouetted by a strident yellow, a complementary bright blue and a tiny note of vibrant green (between her left arm and neck), which is repeated on her right arm but against the blue. Her pale face has touches of orange-brown and the tones of her skin are suggested by quick charcoal hatching and strong notes of white. Despite the glory of all the pastel colours he has used, Degas allows the paper support itself to do much of the work. VH

30 *Woman combing her Hair*

About 1887–90
Charcoal and pastel on paper
55.8 × 27.9 cm
The Burrell Collection, Glasgow
35.237

The subject of a woman combing her hair, or having her hair combed, fascinated Degas. This is one of several works in which he shows a seated or standing naked woman, presumably having taken her bath and having towel-dried her hair and now combing it through. Her face is hidden by her long, chestnut-brown hair, the broad comb and her right hand occupying the place where we would normally expect to see her face. We would also expect her to support her heavy hair with her left hand.

Here Degas enjoys the play of line and form, the cascading lines of her rich brown tresses almost flowing into the draped and heavy damp towel. He has not yet resolved the pose and has experimented with the placing of the towel, which is either draped over or held in her left hand.

The suggestion of a black shadow and the strong, jagged strokes of blue establish her space and emphasise the outline of this slender, flat-stomached figure. The model for this pastel, with her beautiful posture, was surely a ballet dancer. VH

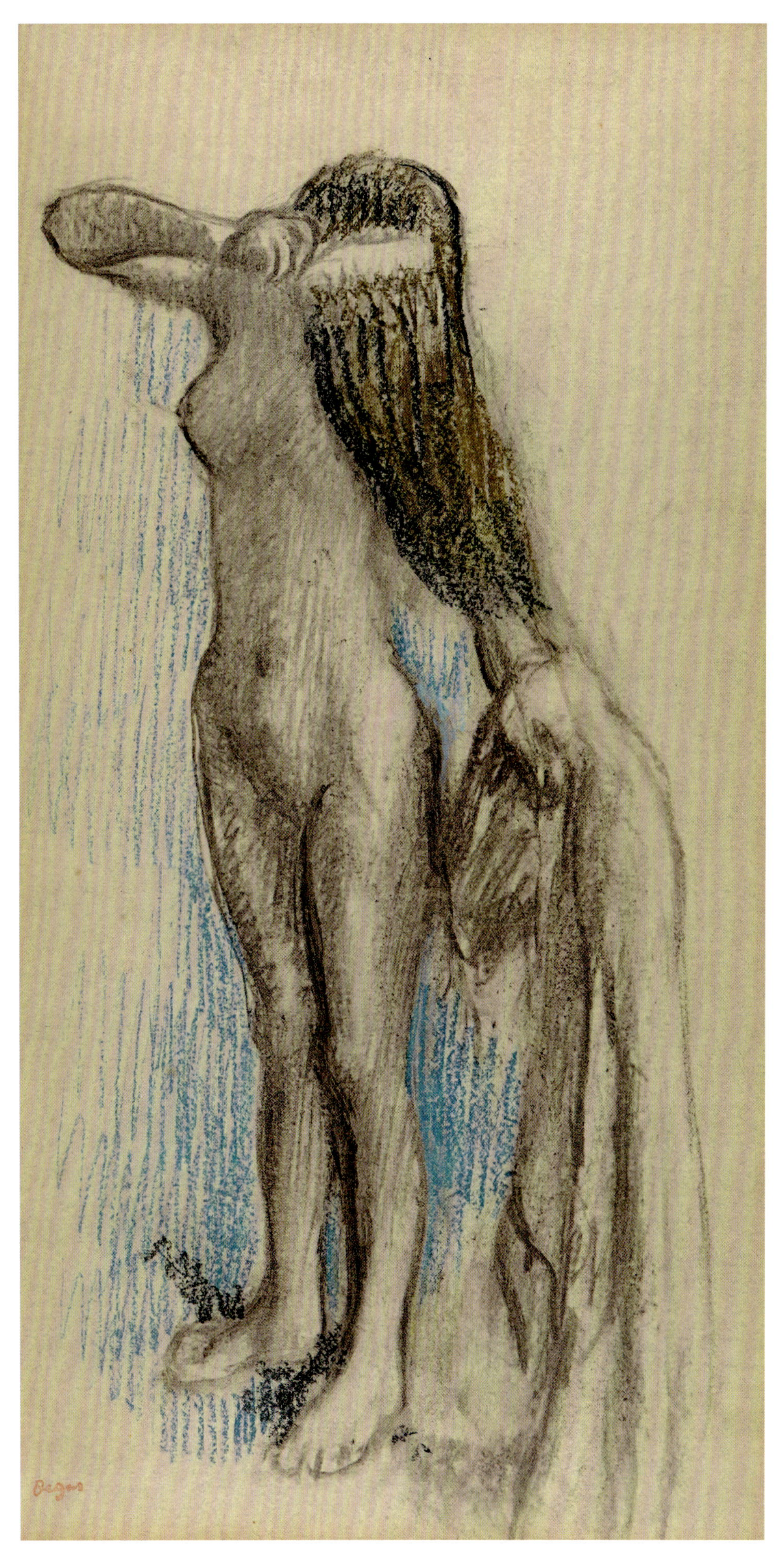
Degas

31 *Combing the Hair*

About 1896
Oil on canvas
114.3 × 146.7 cm
The National Gallery, London
NG 4865

A recurring theme in Degas's work of the 1890s was that of women combing their hair. Here it is a maid who takes on the task; she looks expressionlessly down at the glorious stream of red which she holds with one hand while impassively drawing the comb through. Formally attired in her servant's uniform, she forms a contrast to her still-not-dressed mistress, who, pulled backwards by the force, raises her hand to her head in a gesture of pain or discomfort. A glorious symphony of tones from crimson to scarlet (produced with earths, vermilion and red lead), it is closely related to another painting by Degas of about the same date, *After the Bath (Woman drying herself)* (fig. 6, p. 18), a similar exploration of both physical tension and red tonality.

The composition is sketched in bold sweeps of the brush. While some areas are highly worked, others appear unfinished: objects on the table are sketched in outline only, and features such as the hand raised to head are unresolved. While Degas's attitude to finish was fluid, it does appear that he intended to return to this painting. At some point he enlarged it by placing it on a bigger stretcher, leaving a strip of bare canvas and original stretcher holes exposed at the bottom. But for whatever reason, he never did complete the painting and this was how it appeared at his studio sale in 1918. At some later time it was returned to its original size. Regardless of its degree of finish, however, its magnificent monochromaticity attracted a younger master of colour, Henri Matisse (1869–1954), who acquired it around 1919. SH

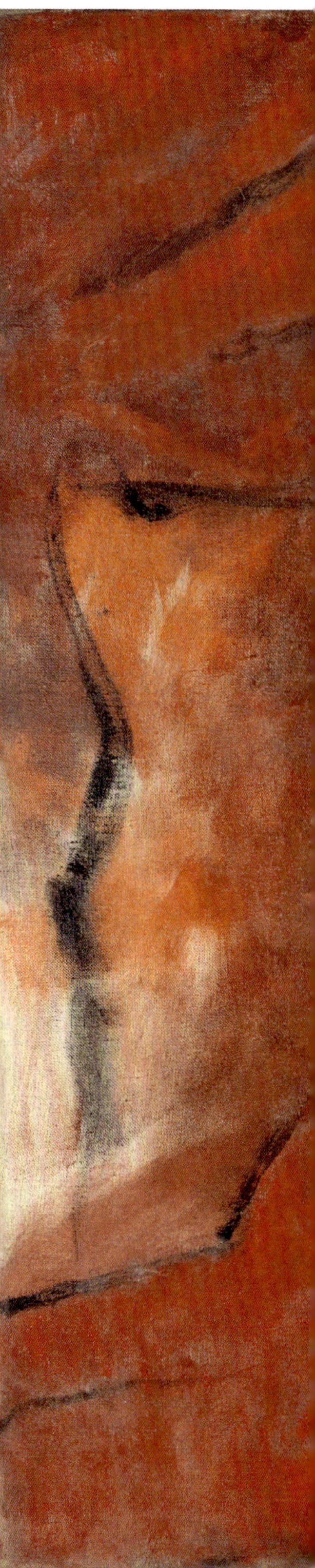

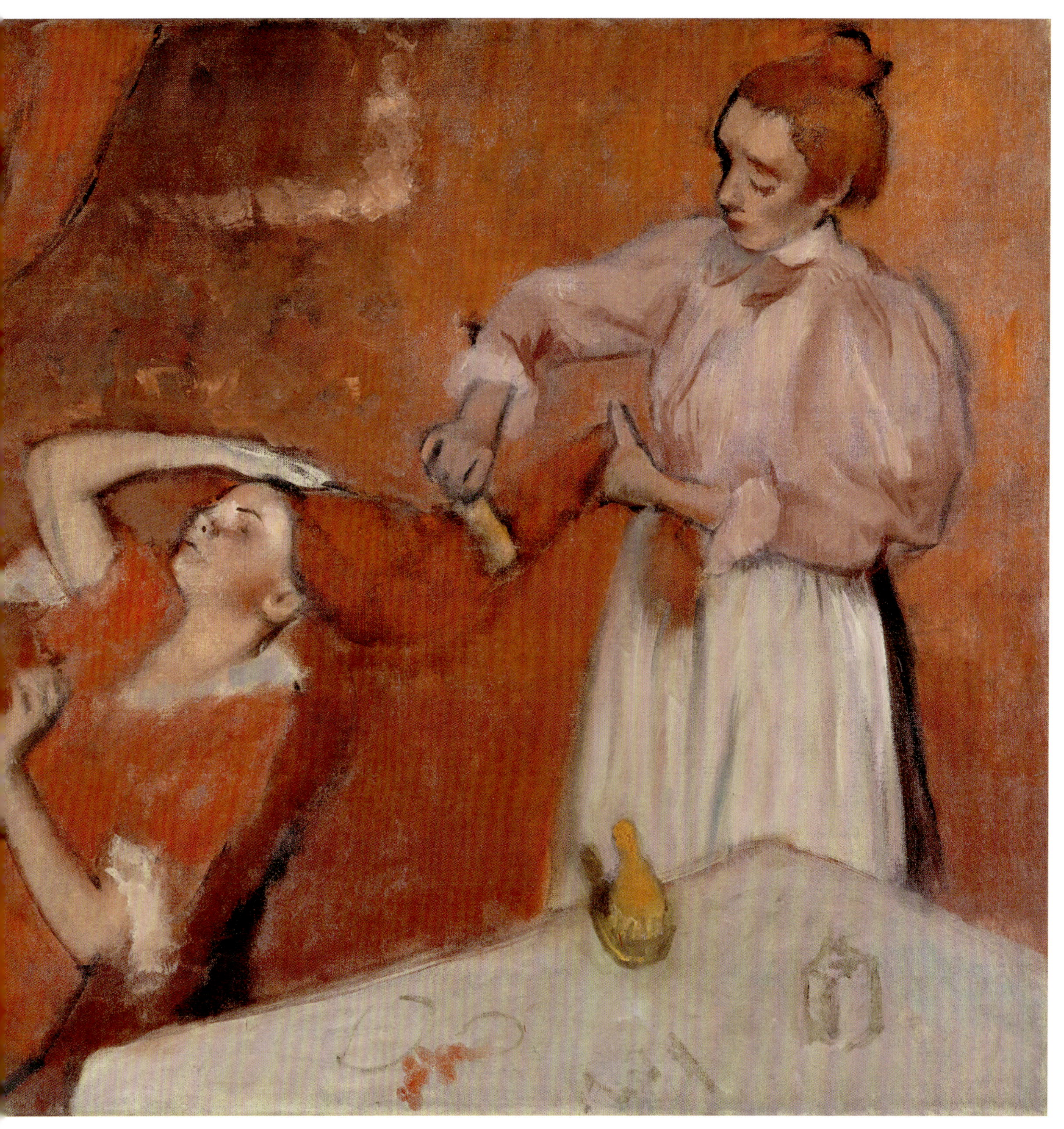

32 *Woman at her Toilette*

About 1897
Pastel on canvas
78.7 × 63.5 cm
The Burrell Collection, Glasgow
35.229

Woman at her Toilette is one of a number of works on this theme that Degas made near the end of his career. This unfinished pastel gives a fascinating insight into how he worked. First he has used charcoal to sketch in the broad outlines of the woman's form and that of the ceramic or metal bowl over which she leans. Next he has blocked in broad areas of pastel – striking and abstract bands of blue, yellow, brown and pink. Unusually, he has chosen to work on an exceptionally coarse canvas rather than paper.

Degas's focus is on the woman's hair and her washing action. We hardly see her face, only the line of her cheek and nose. She is totally absorbed in her task. With just a few, quick strokes of charcoal Degas suggests the fullness of her breasts and the soft folds of skin on her side as she bends forward over the basin.

While we may wonder how far Degas was interested in the erotic connotations of his subject, we can be sure that in this frank depiction of the nude he was fascinated by the abstract play of shapes and forms that it allowed him. Here the bold, exaggerated, deliberate sweep of the woman's hair is echoed by the curve of the bowl, of her right forearm, her breasts, her cheek and the line of hair on her forehead.

In his other treatments of this theme Degas gives more details of the woman's surroundings, such as towels and water jugs, wallpaper, and even a picture or print on the wall behind her. These works are unusual in Degas's representations of the nude as he often conceals the female breast, but here the breasts, supported and emphasised by the washing action, are the focal point of the composition.

One of these pictures is thought to have inspired the Irish novelist George Moore to write: 'I know of a no more degrading spectacle than that of a woman washing herself over a basin; Degas painted it once' (*Mike Fletcher*, 1889). VH

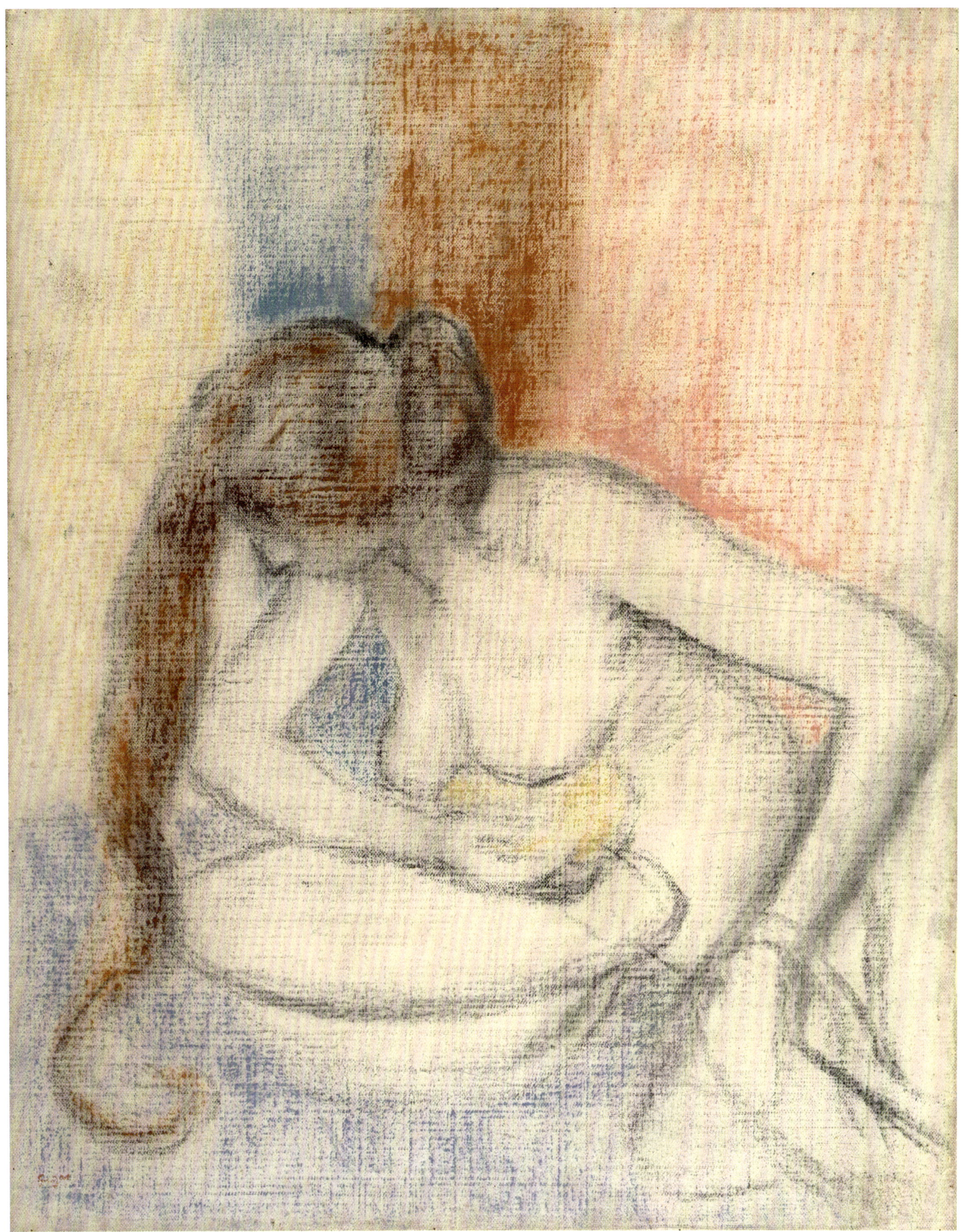

FURTHER READING

These notes are intended to help the reader discover more about Degas's life and art, the works of art illustrated and the ideas discussed in this book. Priority is given to texts in English published relatively recently.

The best **short introduction** to Degas's life and art remains Henri Loyrette's *Degas: The Man and his Art*, New York 1993; while the **most up-to-date survey** of Degas's career can be found in Loyrette's masterly essay for the catalogue of the recent retrospective of the artist's work: *Degas: A New Vision*, exh. cat., Melbourne and Houston 2016–17. The most **comprehensive publication** of Degas's works remains the catalogue of the great 1988–9 monographic exhibition: Jean Sutherland Boggs (ed.), *Degas*, exh. cat., Paris, Ottawa and New York 1988–9. The reference when it comes to dating and identifying most of Degas's pictures is the four-volume **catalogue raisonné** by Paul-André Lemoisne, *Degas et son oeuvre*, Paris 1946.

The main themes of Degas's art have been explored in numerous books and exhibitions over the years. Of those, the following should be singled out: for Degas and other Impressionist artists' interest in **modern life**, see Gary Tinterow and Henri Loyrette (eds), *Origins of Impressionism*, exh. cat., Paris and New York 1994–5. For **portraits**, see Felix Baumann and Marianne Karabelnik (eds), *Degas Portraits*, exh. cat., Zurich and Tübingen 1994–5. For **horseracing** pictures, see Jean Sutherland Boggs (ed.), *Degas at the Races*, exh. cat., Washington 1998. The most thorough analysis of Degas's depiction of the **ballet** and his presence at the Paris Opéra remains Jill DeVonyar and Richard Kendall's *Degas and the Dance*, exh. cat., Detroit and Philadelphia 2002–3; while DeVonyar and Kendall's catalogue of the Royal Academy exhibition *Degas and the Ballet: Picturing Movement*, exh. cat., London 2011, is also excellent. For Degas's **nudes**, see George T.M. Shackelford and Xavier Rey (eds), *Degas and the Nude*, exh. cat., Paris and Boston 2011–12; and Richard Thomson, *Degas: The Nudes*, London 1988. For **landscapes**, see Richard Kendall, *Degas Landscapes*, exh. cat., New York and Houston 1993; and the more recent Ann Dumas et al., *Edgar Degas: The Last Landscapes*, exh. cat., Columbus and Copenhagen 2006–7.

Similarly, Degas's work in media other than oil has been the subject of various monographic publications and exhibitions. For **pastels**, see Jean Sutherland Boggs and Anne Maheux, *Degas Pastels*, New York 1992. For **drawings**, see Jean Sutherland Boggs, *Drawings by Degas*, exh. cat., Saint Louis 1966. A more recent publication on Degas's graphic oeuvre in pastel and drawing is Christopher Lloyd's *Edgar Degas: Drawings and Pastels*, London 2014. For **prints**, see the excellent catalogue of the recent milestone exhibition at the Museum of Modern Art, New York: Jodi Hauptman (ed.), *Degas: A Strange New Beauty*, exh. cat., New York 2016. For Degas's **sculptures**, see Susan Glover Lindsay, Daphne S. Barbour and Shelley G. Sturman (eds), *Edgar Degas Sculpture*, Washington 2010; and Joseph S. Czestochowski and Anne Pingeot, *Degas Sculptures: Catalogue Raisonné of the Bronzes*, New York and Memphis 2002. Discussions of Degas's **photographs** are peppered throughout most of the recent literature, but a good reference is Malcolm R. Daniel's *Edgar Degas, Photographer*, exh. cat., New York, Los Angeles and Paris 1998–9.

A thorough examination of Degas's **techniques** in various media seen through pictures in the National Gallery collection can be found in David Bomford et al., *Art in the Making: Degas*, exh. cat., London 2004–5. A recent publication by the National Gallery of Art, Washington, Daphne Barbour and Suzanne Quillen Lomax (eds), *Facture: Conservation, Science, Art History*, vol. 3: *Degas*, Washington 2017, offers new insights into Degas's technique in a wide range of media. For additional observations on Degas's pastel methods and materials, see Anne Maheux, *Degas Pastels*, exh. cat., Ottawa 1988; Denis Rouart, *Degas in Search of his Technique*, trans. Pia DeSantis, New York 1988; and Richard Kendall's catalogue for the National Gallery exhibition *Degas: Beyond Impressionism*, exh. cat., London and Chicago 1996–7.

An important work on the **social and historical context** of painting in Paris in the second half of the nineteenth century remains T.J. Clark's *The Painting of Modern Life*, Princeton 1984. An equally fascinating and less polemical survey can be found in Henri Loyrette, Sébastien Allard and Laurence des Cars, *Nineteenth Century French Art*, Paris 2007. On the topic of Degas's **representations of women** and accusations of **misogyny**, a good introduction remains Norma Broude's 'Degas's "Misogyny"', *The Art Bulletin*, vol. 59, no. 1 (March 1977), pp. 95–107. A fascinating collection of essays on the topic can be found in Richard Kendall and Griselda Pollock (eds), *Dealing with Degas: Representations of Women and the Politics of Vision*, London 1992. On Degas's **artistic legacy and influence**, see Kendall's *Degas: Beyond Impressionism* and Jane Munro (ed.), *Degas: A Passion for Perfection*, exh. cat., Cambridge and Denver 2017–18.

Degas was an intensely private man. His **personal life** mostly eluded his contemporaries as it still does researchers a century after his death. Sue Roe's *The Private Lives of the Impressionists*, London 2006, offers a fascinating insight into the lives of nineteenth-century painters, including Degas. **Degas's own writings** are rich and varied, but contain relatively few references to his art. Richard Kendall (ed.), *Degas by Himself: Drawings, Prints, Paintings, Writings*, London 1987, offers a generous selection of Degas's correspondence as well a variety of **second-hand accounts**, recollections of people who came across him, such as his friends the Rouarts and his dealer Ambroise Vollard. Degas was a witty and incisive conversationalist and recollections of encounters at dinner parties or at his studio can offer penetrating insights into his artistic practice. The final chapter of Henri Loyrette's *Degas: The Man and his Art* offers another short but fascinating selection of writings by people who encountered Degas. Paul Valéry's essay *Degas Danse Dessin* of 1936 must be singled out; it was translated by David Paul in *The Collected Works of Paul Valéry: Degas, Manet, Morisot*, Princeton 1989. **Diaries** of contemporaries, such as Julie Manet, are particularly enlightening. A new edition and translation by Jane Roberts, *Growing Up with the Impressionists: The Diary of Julie Manet* will be published in 2017.

An introduction to Degas's **collecting** can be found in Anne Robbins's essay in *Painters' Paintings*, exh. cat., London 2016. For a thorough study of his collection, see Ann Dumas (ed.), *The Private Collection of Edgar Degas*, exh. cat., New York 1997–8; while *The Private Collection of Edgar Degas: A Summary Catalogue*, New York 1997, compiled by Colta Feller Ives et al., contains information on the more than five thousand works Degas owned. On the **Parisian art trade** in the nineteenth century more generally, see Sylvie Patry (ed.), *Inventing Impressionism: Paul Durand-Ruel and the Modern Art Market*, exh. cat., Paris, London and Philadelphia 2014–15. For a readable and beautifully illustrated account of **collectors and collecting in Scotland** see Frances Fowle, *Impressionism and Scotland*, Edinburgh 2008. For a revealing insight into the dealer who influenced taste in Scotland, see Frances Fowle's *Van Gogh's Twin: The Scottish Art Dealer Alexander Reid*, Edinburgh 2010. The best introduction to **William Burrell**'s life and collecting is Richard Marks, *Burrell: A Portrait of a Collector, Sir William Burrell 1861–1958*, Glasgow 1983. An entertaining and highly informative account of Burrell and other west of Scotland collectors was written by the former director of Glasgow Museums, T.J.Honeyman: *Art and Audacity*, London 1971.

Finally, for those wanting to turn to **literature**, key works of nineteenth-century French literature relating to art include – in translation – Honoré De Balzac, *The Unknown Masterpiece*, New York 1831 (2000); Emile Zola, *The Masterpiece*, Oxford 1886 (2008); and Charles Baudelaire, *The Painter of Modern Life*, London 1863 (2010). A beautiful, vivid re-creation of the world of Baudelaire and his artist contemporaries including Degas can be found in Roberto Calasso's *La Folie Baudelaire*, London 2012. James Fenton's *Leonardo's Nephew: Essays on Art and Artists*, Chicago 1998, contains two fascinating and evocative chapters on Degas: the incriminating story of a dinner in 1907 when Harry Graf Kessler met the ageing and now insufferable artist, and the story of the sale of Degas's collection after his death. JD

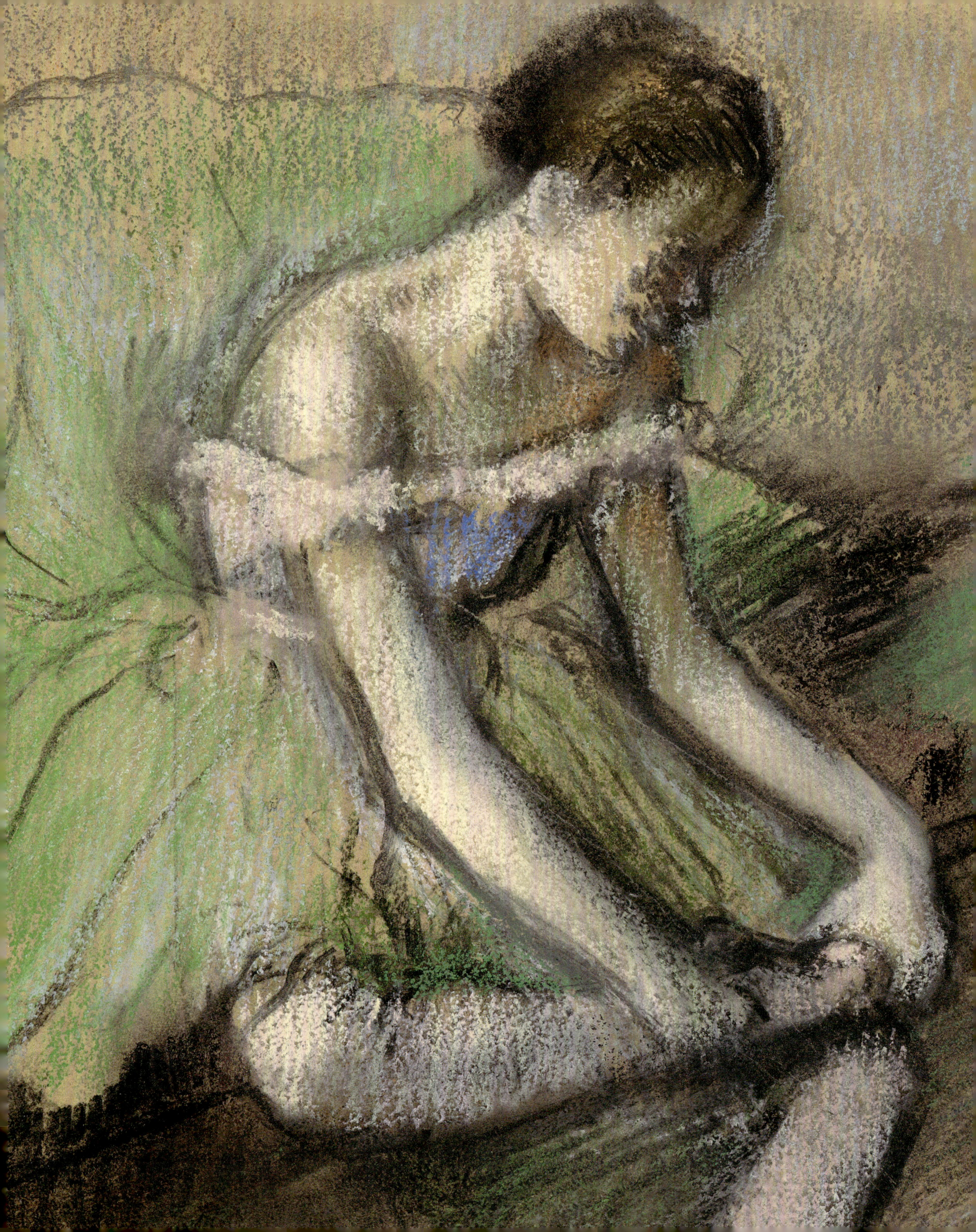

LIST OF LENDERS

Berwick-upon-Tweed
Berwick-upon-Tweed Museum & Art Gallery

Glasgow, The Burrell Collection
Lent by Glasgow Life (Glasgow Museums) on behalf of Glasgow City Council: from the Burrell Collection with the approval of the Burrell Trustees

Glasgow, Kelvingrove Art Gallery and Museum
Lent by Glasgow Life (Glasgow Museums) on behalf of Glasgow City Council

London
The National Gallery

PHOTOGRAPHIC CREDITS

Geneva
Graphic Arts Cabinet of the Museums of Art and History, Geneva © Musées d'art et d'histoire, Ville de Genève, Cabinet d'arts graphiques, legs Edouard Sarasin, no. inv. 1917-0027. Photo: Bettina Jacot-Descombes: fig. 14.

Berwick-upon-Tweed
© Berwick Museum & Art Gallery: cat. 21.

Dallas
© Dallas Museum of Art, Texas, USA / gift of Mr and Mrs Franklin B. Bartholow / Bridgeman Images: fig. 9.

Glasgow
The Burrell Collection, Glasgow © CSG CIC Glasgow Museums Collection: cats 1, 2, 3, 4, 6, 7, 9, 10, 11, 12, 15, 16, 17, 18, 19, 23, 24, 25, 28, 29, 30, 32; figs 7, 8, 12, 13, 16, 17; p. 44. Glasgow Museums: Art Gallery & Museums, Kelvingrove © CSG CIC Glasgow Museums Collection: cats 13, 20.

London
© The National Gallery, London: cats 8, 14, 22, 26, 27, 31; fig. 1.

Los Angeles
© The J. Paul Getty Museum, Los Angeles, California: fig. 5.

Paris
Musée d'Orsay, Paris © Musée d'Orsay, Dist. RMN-Grand Palais / Patrice Schmidt: figs 2, 3; © RMN-Grand Palais (musée d'Orsay) / Hervé Lewandowski: fig. 4.

Philadelphia
© Philadelphia Museum of Art, Pennsylvania: fig. 6.

Private collection
© Christie's Images / Bridgeman Images: figs 10, 11, 15.
© Private collection 2000. Used by permission: cat. 5.

Washington, DC
National Gallery of Art, Washington, DC, Image courtesy of the Board of Trustees, National Gallery of Art, Washington, DC: figs 18, 19.

ACKNOWLEDGEMENTS

The authors would like to thank Martin Bellamy, Alan Broadfoot, Tarn Brown, Caroline Campbell, Ulrika Danielsson, Sarah Derry, Raymond Docherty, Gabriele Finaldi, Charlotte Gere, Allison Goudie, Jan Green, Stewart Grimshaw, Lynne Harrison, Jane Hyne, Leah Kharibian, Maureen Kinnear, Jane Knowles, Anna Koopstra, Rosalind McKever, Lizzie Marx, Morna Mathers, Nicholas Penny, Anne Robbins, James Robinson, Lucian Robinson, Otto Saumarez Smith, Peter Schade, Mark Slattery, Johanna Stephenson, Winnie Tyrrell, Raymonde Watkins, Francesca Whitlum-Cooper and Félix Zorzo.

Sponsored by

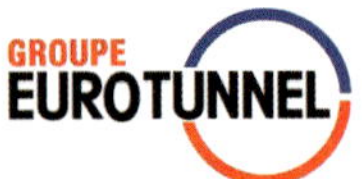

Exhibition generously supported by
The Elizabeth Cayzer Charitable Trust
Colin Clark

Published to accompany the exhibition
Drawn in Colour: Degas from the Burrell
The National Gallery, London
20 September 2017–30 April 2018

Curated by Julien Domercq, with Christopher Riopelle

This exhibition has been made possible by the provision of insurance through the Government Indemnity Scheme. The National Gallery would like to thank HM Government for providing Government Indemnity and the Department for Culture, Media and Sport and Arts Council England for arranging the indemnity.

First published in 2017 by
National Gallery Company Limited
St Vincent House
30 Orange Street
London WC2H 7HH
www.nationalgallery.co.uk

ISBN 978 1 85709 625 5

British Library Cataloguing-in-Publication Data
A catalogue record is available from the British Library

Library of Congress Control Number 2017939574

All measurements give height before width

PUBLISHER Jan Green
PROJECT EDITOR Sarah Derry
EDITOR Johanna Stephenson
DESIGNER Raymonde Watkins
PRODUCTION Jane Hyne and Amanda Mackie
PICTURE RESEARCHER Félix Zorzo

Printed in Italy by Verona Libri

COVER Detail from *Dancer adjusting her Shoulder Strap* (cat. 29)
FRONTISPIECE Detail from *The Red Ballet Skirts* (cat. 19)
PAGE 4 Detail from *After the Bath, Woman drying herself* (cat. 27)
PAGE 6 Detail from *The Rehearsal* (cat. 11)
PAGE 110 Detail from *The Green Ballet Skirt* (cat. 18)

Vivien Hamilton is Research Manager, Art, Glasgow Museums

Julien Domercq is Vivmar Curatorial Fellow at the National Gallery, London

Harriet K. Stratis is Senior Research Conservator at the Art Institute of Chicago

Christopher Riopelle is Curator of Post-1800 Paintings at the National Gallery, London

Sarah Herring is Isaiah Berlin Associate Curator of Post-1800 Paintings at the National Gallery, London